1st EDITION

Perspectives on Diseases and Disorders

Heart Disease

Clay Farris Naff

Book Editor

PERSPECTIVES
On Diseases & Disorders

GALE
CENGAGE Learning

Detroit • New York • San Francisco • New Haven, Conn • Waterville, Maine • London

GALE
CENGAGE Learning

Christine Nasso, *Publisher*
Elizabeth Des Chenes, *Managing Editor*

© 2008 Greenhaven Press, a part of Gale, Cengage Learning

Gale and Greenhaven Press are registered trademarks used herein under license.

For more information, contact:
Greenhaven Press
27500 Drake Rd.
Farmington Hills, MI 48331-3535
Or you can visit our Internet site at gale.cengage.com

For product information and technology assistance, contact us at

Gale Customer Support, 1-800-877-4253
For permission to use material from this text or product, submit all requests online at www.cengage.com/permissions

Further permissions questions can be emailed to permissionrequest@cengage.com

Articles in Greenhaven Press anthologies are often edited for length to meet page requirements. In addition, original titles of these works are changed to clearly present the main thesis and to explicitly indicate the author's opinion. Every effort is made to ensure that Greenhaven Press accurately reflects the original intent of the authors. Every effort has been made to trace the owners of copyrighted material.

Cover image copyright Sebastian Kaulitzki, 2008. Used under license from Shutterstock.com.

LIBRARY OF CONGRESS CATALOGING-IN-PUBLICATION DATA

Heart disease / Clay Farris Naff, book editor.
      p. cm. — (Perspectives on diseases and disorders)
   Includes bibliographical references and index.
   ISBN: 978-0-7377-4026-4 (hardcover)
   1. Heart—Diseases—Popular works. I. Naff, Clay Farris.
   RC681.H35 2008
   616.1'2—dc22   2008006491

Printed in the United States of America
1 2 3 4 5 6 7 12 11 10 09 08

CONTENTS

clogged coronary arteries, which threaten to choke off the heart's blood supply. Other medical imaging methods may also be useful.

CHAPTER 3   Personal Experiences of Heart Disease

INTRODUCTION

The heart is the body's most powerful organ, both physically and symbolically. It pumps approximately one hundred thousand times a day, every day, for a lifetime. Unlike any other muscle in the body, the heart never rests except for the momentary lull between one beat and the next.

The heart is a symbol of power, emotion, compassion, and love. To the ancient Egyptians, the heart was the seat of the soul. To ancient Greek physicians, it was the center of all emotions. In Catholicism, the heart remains the symbol of sacred compassion. In contemporary American culture, the heart symbolizes love. In short, there is no more potent symbol. However, when the heart becomes diseased, it threatens life itself. Indeed, heart disease is by far the number one cause of death in the United States.

Long Climb to Comprehension

Knowledge about heart disease has been hard won. It took thousands of years to arrive at a scientific understanding of the heart. Its function may seem obvious now, but for thousands of years it was deeply misunderstood. Medieval medicine held that the heart was the body's engine of heat. When in 1616 English physician William Harvey discovered the circulation of blood, he had to fight against millennia of dogmatic belief to get his ideas accepted.

Well into the twentieth century, mistaken ideas about heart disease prevailed, even among experts. During the 1940s, for example, more than one hundred thousand U.S. doctors recommended smoking Camel cigarettes for health. It is now well established that smoking, with all its other risks, directly promotes heart disease. The role of cholesterol as a cause of heart disease was suspected as early as 1856, but scientific consensus on the issue only emerged in 1984. Since then, dramatic improvements in the understanding and treatment of heart disease have been achieved.

Causes of Heart Disease

Infectious diseases, such as the common cold, are easily explained in terms of their proximate (or immediate) cause. If a rhinovirus makes its way into the body and succeeds in replicating itself, a head cold will develop. It is that simple.

Heart disease is far more complex. To understand it, it is necessary to look at both proximate and ultimate causes. The proximate cause of a heart attack is most often a clot or clog in one of the major blood vessels that supplies the heart. Cut off from oxygen and nutrients, the heart immediately begins to falter, and unless the clog is dislodged death may follow within minutes. Other varieties of heart disease may also be explained in terms of proximate causes. A faulty heart valve may lead to blood pooling in a chamber when it is supposed to be pumped out, and the entire rhythm of the heart may be thrown off stride, like a marching band stumbling over a fallen player, with disastrous consequences. Or again, a portion of the heart muscle may decay, weakening the ability of the entire organ to pump blood.

However, all of these versions of heart disease require further explanation in terms of ultimate causes. It is in this arena that medical knowledge has been rapidly growing. If a proximate cause is the closest to the actual situation, the most remote ultimate cause of heart disease is genetics. People inherit genes from their parents that make them more or less vulnerable to heart disease. Genes by themselves do not cause heart disease, but under certain circumstances—in the presence, say, of a certain level of hormones in the womb—a genetic predisposition can lead to a congenital heart defect. A tragic result is that some otherwise healthy young people—including gifted athletes—die of heart failure in the prime of life.

However, natural selection ensures that such youthful consequences are rare (people with genes that set them up for early heart failure rarely have a chance to pass them on to the next generation). All the same, researchers have found that genes play a role in the vulnerability of older people to heart disease. For example, some people are genetically predisposed to experience elevated blood pressure as they age. High blood pressure puts a strain on the heart and may weaken it to a dangerous degree. That is one reason why doctors now routinely ask patients whether their parents or other family members have high blood pressure.

A major cause of heart disease is lifestyle. People whose diets are high in meat and dairy products ingest a lot of cholesterol (on top of that which their bodies manufacture). Low-density cholesterol, a sticky substance that circulates in the bloodstream, tends to clog arteries. It has emerged as a key factor in reducing the blood supply to the heart and triggering heart attacks. Awareness of this threat has led the medical community to advise people to trim the amount of cholesterol-laden red meat in their diets and to get regular exercise, which can reduce the proportion of low-density cholesterol in their bloodstreams.

Recent research has begun to uncover additional ultimate causes of heart disease. Stress hormones may be one. These are hormones generated by the body under stressful circumstances. In the short term, their function is to stimulate inflammation in various muscles, perhaps to facilitate a getaway response or to activate the immune system. However, modern life, with its lengthy traffic jams, loud noises, and numerous frustrations, causes

A high level of stress can increase the risk of heart disease. (AP Images.)

many people to experience chronic, almost constant, stress. The result may be gradual damage to the heart.

Another possibility under investigation is bacteria. Specifically, some evidence suggests that the bacteria implicated in tooth decay may also be responsible for damage to the heart. It might seem improbable at first that something a dentist treats could have an influence on the heart, but this would not be the first bacterial surprise. For many years, doctors believed that stomach ulcers were caused by stress. In the 1990s, however, researchers learned that the principal cause was a bacterium that had evolved to live in the stomach's harsh environment and that fed off the protective lining of the stomach, eventually exposing the skin underneath to digestive acids. A simple regimen of antibiotics eliminated the threat for millions of people.

Treatment and Prevention

The treatment of heart disease by medicines and other methods continues to develop rapidly. Statins, a class of drugs that reduce the production of cholesterol in the body, have been widely prescribed, and while their use under some circumstances can be controversial, no one doubts that they have saved lives by preventing heart attacks. When heart attacks strike, clot-busting drugs, including aspirin, now save many lives. So, too, do automatic defibrillators, machines that use electric shocks to restore rhythm to a malfunctioning heart.

The most drastic treatment for heart disease is the heart transplant. Pioneered by South African surgeon Christiaan Barnard in 1967, it has become a common, if not exactly routine, operation. However, anyone who undergoes a heart transplant is fated to spend the rest of his or her life on a regimen of immunosuppressant drugs to prevent the body from attacking the organ replacement. This exposes the patient to a much greater risk from infectious disease.

One treatment that may become feasible in the future is replacement of a diseased heart with a mechanical substitute. Heart surgeon Robert Jarvik has led the way on this front, and his design has proven capable of sustaining a patient's life for months beyond when it would have otherwise ended. However, the technology has severe limitations, and terminally ill heart patients who have undergone experimental heart replacements have arguably had little quality of life afterward.

Dr. Robert Jarvik holds up the "Jarvik 2000," an artificial heart he designed. (**AP Images.**)

The consensus among those who study heart disease is to endorse the old saying, "An ounce of prevention is worth a pound of cure." Congenital heart disease may require intervention, and some people will always need long-term drug therapy to keep their cholesterol level or blood pressure down, but an effort to lead a healthy lifestyle based on a sensible diet, regular exercise, and management of stress is the least costly and most promising way to stave off heart disease.

CHAPTER 1

Understanding Heart Disease

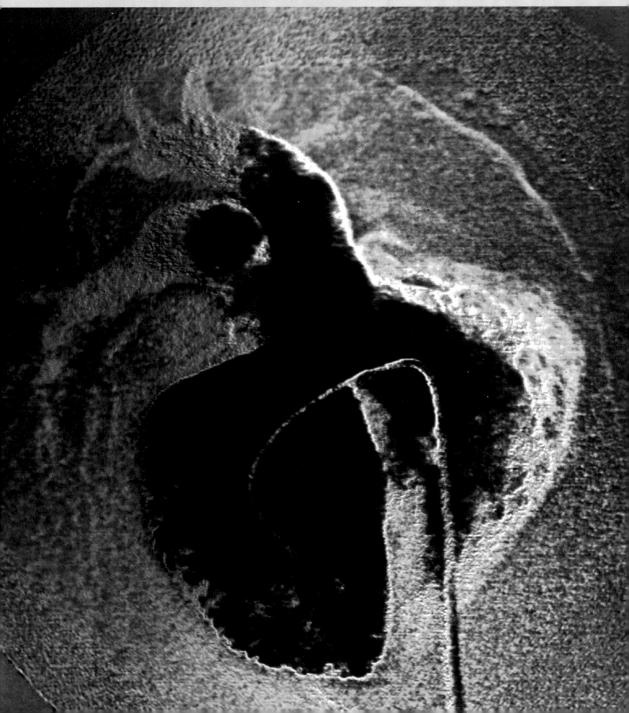

America's Leading Killer

World of Health

Heart disease leads all other causes of death in America. Contrary to stereotype, it strikes women as well as men, youth as well as the elderly. In the following selection the editors of Gale's *World of Health* examine coronary heart disease, the type that most often proves fatal. The heart is a powerful muscle that beats roughly one hundred thousand times a day. It requires a constant supply of oxygen-rich blood for fuel. Coronary heart disease results from a blockage of the arteries that supply the heart with that blood. The blockages typically come about from an accumulation of cholesterol on the walls of the arteries. New diagnosis and treatment techniques are helping to cut the death rate from coronary heart disease, but it remains America's leading killer. Gale's *World of Health* is a single-volume publication designed for high school students to enable them to grasp the societal implications of human health, disease, and medical practice throughout history.

Photo on previous page. This angiogram shows a catheter inserted into a heart with a ventricular septal defect (VSD), or a defect in the wall separating the left and right sides of the heart. VSDs are a common form of congenital heart disease. (Copyright Simon Fraser/SPL/Photo Researchers, Inc. Reproduced by permission.)

SOURCE: *World of Health*, Detroit, MI: Gale, 2007. Copyright © 2007 Cengage Learning, Gale. Reproduced by permission of Gale, a part of Cengage Learning.

Coronary artery disease, also called coronary heart disease or heart disease, is the leading cause of death for both men and women in the United States and Europe. The American Heart Association states that during the year 2003, about 13.2 million people in the United States had coronary heart disease. However, with improved treatment options and advances in drugs, the number of deaths from coronary artery disease continues to decline.

Coronary artery disease occurs when the coronary arteries become partially blocked or clogged. This blockage limits the flow of blood from the coronary arteries, the major arteries supplying oxygen-rich blood to the heart. The coronary arteries expand when the heart is working harder and needs more oxygen. If the arteries are unable to expand, the heart is deprived of oxygen (myocardial ischemia). When the blockage is limited, chest pain or pressure called angina may occur. When the blockage cuts off the flow of blood, the result is heart attack (myocardial infarction or heart muscle death).

Healthy coronary arteries are clean, smooth, and slick. The artery walls are flexible and can expand to let more blood through when the heart needs to work harder. The disease process in arteries is thought to begin with an injury to the linings and walls of the arteries. This injury makes them susceptible to atherosclerosis and blood clots (thrombosis).

FAST FACT

Although heart disease is the leading cause of death among both men and women, at least 70 percent of sudden heart attacks occur in men.

Clogs Block Arteries

Coronary artery disease is usually caused by atherosclerosis. Cholesterol and other fatty substances accumulate on the inner wall of the arteries. They attract fibrous tissue, blood components, and calcium and harden into artery-clogging plaques. Atherosclerotic plaques often form blood clots that can also block the coronary arteries (coronary thrombosis). Congenital defects and muscle spasms, too, can block blood flow. Recent research indicates that infection from organisms such as chlamydia bacteria may be responsible for some cases of coronary artery disease.

A number of major contributing factors increase the risk of developing coronary artery disease. Some of these can be changed and some cannot. People with more risk factors are more likely to develop coronary artery disease.

Risk factors that cannot be changed include heredity, sex, and age. For example, people whose parents have

In this illustration, cholesterol and other fatty substances have accumulated on the inner wall of an artery, restricting blood flow. (3D Clinic/Getty Images.)

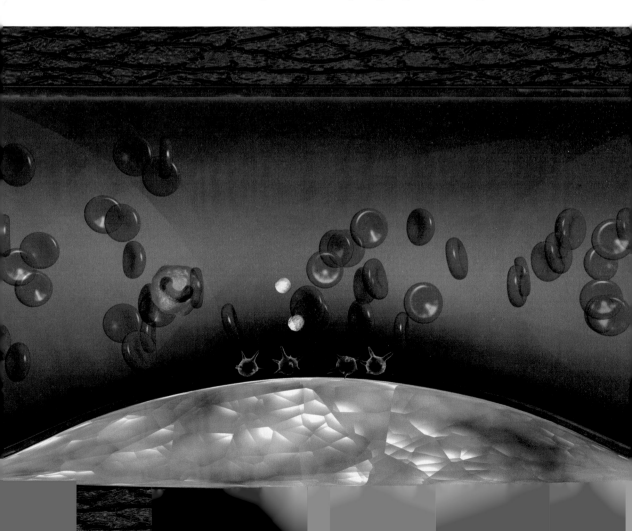

coronary artery disease are more likely to develop it. African-Americans are also at increased risk because they experience a higher rate of severe hypertension than do whites. Men are more likely to have heart attacks than women are and to have them at a younger age. Over age 60 years, however, women have coronary artery disease at a rate equal to that of men. Occasionally, coronary disease may strike a person in the thirties. Older people (those over 65 years) are more likely to die of a heart attack. Older women are twice as likely as older men to die within a few weeks of a heart attack.

Smoking Heightens Risk

Other risk factors can be changed. For example, smoking increases both the chance of developing coronary artery disease and the chance of dying from it. Smokers are two to four times more likely than are nonsmokers to die of sudden heart attack. Second-hand smoke may also increase risk, as can dietary sources of cholesterol including meat, eggs, and other animal products. The body also produces it. Age, sex, heredity, and diet affect one's blood cholesterol. The risk of developing coronary artery disease increases steadily as blood cholesterol levels increase above 160 mg/dL (milligrams per deciliter). When a person has other risk factors, the risk multiplies.

High blood pressure makes the heart work harder and weakens it over time. It increases the risk of heart attack, stroke, kidney failure, and congestive heart failure. In combination with obesity, smoking, high cholesterol, or diabetes, high blood pressure raises the risk of heart attack or stroke several times.

Lack of exercise increases the risk of coronary artery disease. Even modest physical activity, like walking, is beneficial if done regularly.

The risk of developing coronary artery disease is seriously increased for diabetics. More than 80% of diabetics die of some type of heart or blood vessel disease.

Other risk factors such as obesity, stress, and anger have been linked to coronary artery disease, but their significance is not known yet.

Chest pain (angina) is the main symptom of coronary heart disease, but it is not always present. Other symptoms include shortness of breath, and chest heaviness, tightness, pain, a burning sensation, squeezing, or pressure either behind the breastbone or in the arms, neck, or jaws. Many people have no symptoms of coronary artery disease before having a heart attack.

Means of Diagnosis

Diagnostic tests for coronary artery disease measure weight, blood pressure, blood lipid levels, and fasting blood glucose levels (blood sugar, an indicator of diabetes). Other diagnostic tests help to confirm the diagnosis.

An electrocardiogram (ECG) shows the heart's activity and may reveal a lack of oxygen (ischemia). However, a definite diagnosis cannot be made from electrocardiography. About 50% of patients with significant coronary artery disease have normal resting electrocardiograms. Another type of electrocardiogram is known as the exercise stress test. It measures how the heart and blood vessels respond to exertion when the patient is exercising on a treadmill or a stationary bike. However, it sometimes gives a normal reading when the patient has a heart problem or an abnormal reading when the patient does not.

If the electrocardiogram reveals a problem or is inconclusive, the next step is exercise echocardiography or nuclear scanning (angiography), which uses sound waves to create an image of the heart's chambers and valves. It does not reveal the coronary arteries themselves but can detect abnormalities in heart wall motion caused by coronary disease.

Radionuclide angiography enables physicians to see the blood flow of the coronary arteries. Nuclear scans are performed by injecting a small amount of a radiophar-

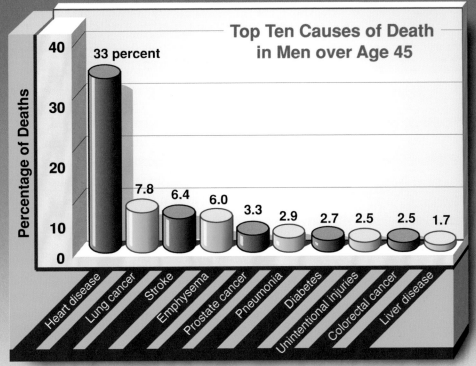

The Number One Killer of Middle-Aged Men

Top Ten Causes of Death in Men over Age 45

Percentage of Deaths

- Heart disease: 33 percent
- Lung cancer: 7.8
- Stroke: 6.4
- Emphysema: 6.0
- Prostate cancer: 3.3
- Pneumonia: 2.9
- Diabetes: 2.7
- Unintentional injuries: 2.5
- Colorectal cancer: 2.5
- Liver disease: 1.7

Taken from: U.S. Department of Health and Human Services, Centers for Disease Control and Prevention.

maceutical (a radioactive chemical) such as thallium into the bloodstream. A scanning camera passes back and forth over the patient who lies on a table. Thallium scanning is usually done in conjunction with an exercise stress test. When the stress test is finished, thallium or sestamibi is injected. The patient resumes exercise for one minute to absorb the thallium.

Coronary angiography is the most accurate method for making a diagnosis of coronary artery disease, but it is also the most invasive. As a form of cardiac catheterization, it shows the heart's chambers, great vessels, and coronary arteries using x-ray technology.

Variety of Treatments

Coronary artery disease can be treated many ways. The choice of treatment depends on the severity of the disease. Treatments include lifestyle changes and drug therapy, percutaneous [skin-penetrating] transluminal coronary angioplasty, and coronary artery bypass surgery. Coronary artery disease is a chronic disease requiring life-long care. Angioplasty or bypass surgery is not a cure.

People with less severe coronary artery disease may gain adequate control through lifestyle changes and drug therapy. Many of the lifestyle changes that prevent disease progression—a low-fat, low-cholesterol diet; weight loss if needed; exercise; and not smoking—also help prevent the disease from developing.

Drugs such as nitrates, beta-blockers, and calcium-channel blockers relieve chest pain and complications of coronary artery disease, but they cannot clear blocked arteries. Nitrates (nitroglycerin) improve blood flow to the heart. Beta-blockers (acebutelol, propranolol) reduce the amount of oxygen required by the heart during stress. One type of calcium-channel blocker (Verapamil, diltiazem hydrochloride) helps keep the arteries open and reduces blood pressure. Aspirin helps prevent blood clots from forming on plaques, reducing the likelihood of a heart attack. Cholesterol-lowering medications are also indicated in most cases.

Percutaneous transluminal coronary angioplasty and bypass surgery are procedures that enter the body (invasive procedures) to improve blood flow in the coronary arteries [by using a probe to clear out clogs]. Percutaneous transluminal coronary angioplasty, usually called coronary angioplasty, is a non-surgical procedure. It is successful about 90% of the time, but for one-third of patients the artery narrows again within six months. The procedure can be repeated. It is less invasive and less expensive than coronary artery bypass surgery.

In coronary artery bypass surgery, a healthy artery or vein from an arm, leg, or chest wall is used to build a detour around the coronary artery blockage. The healthy vessel then supplies oxygen-rich blood to the heart. Bypass surgery is major surgery. It is appropriate for those patients with blockages in two or three major coronary arteries, those with severely narrowed left main coronary arteries, and those who have not responded to other treatments.

Three semi-experimental surgical procedures for unblocking coronary arteries are currently being studied. Atherectomy is a procedure in which the cardiologist shaves off and removes strips of plaque from the blocked artery. In laser angioplasty, a catheter with a laser tip is inserted into the affected artery to burn or break down the plaque. A metal coil called a stent can be implanted permanently to keep a blocked artery open. Stenting is becoming more common.

Mortality Rate Down

In many cases, coronary artery disease can be successfully treated. Advances in medicine and healthier lifestyles have caused a substantial decline in death rates from coronary artery disease since the mid-1980s. New diagnostic techniques enable doctors to identify and treat coronary artery disease in its earliest stages. New technologies and surgical procedures have extended the lives of many patients who would otherwise have died. Research on coronary artery disease continues.

A healthy lifestyle can help prevent coronary artery disease and help keep it from progressing. A heart-healthy lifestyle includes eating a healthy diet, getting regular exercise, maintaining a healthy weight, not smoking, drinking alcohol in moderate amounts or not at all, not taking recreational drugs, controlling hypertension, and managing stress. Cardiac rehabilitation programs work very well to help prevent recurring coronary problems for people who are at risk and who have already had coronary events and procedures.

Heart Disease Hits Women Harder

Roni Rabin

The stereotype of a heart-attack victim is invariably male. For many years the medical profession also believed that heart disease was primarily a danger to men. In the following selection journalist Roni Rabin explodes the stereotypes. While it remains true that younger heart-disease victims are predominantly male, postmenopausal women are at virtually the same risk. What is more, women who do suffer from heart disease are more likely to die of it, Rabin reports. Doctors are puzzled about why that is the case. Some think it has to do with smaller blood vessels in women. Others think there may be disparities in research and treatment of women's heart disease. Whatever the cause, doctors now advise women to pay attention to their heart health. Rabin is a staff writer for the Long Island, New York–based publication *Newsday*.

It seems incongruous, to say the least: Women, who survive labor pain and childrearing and still usually outlive men, are more likely to die after a heart attack.

SOURCE: Roni Rabin, "The Gender Gap," *Newsday*, February 2005. Copyright © 2005 Newsday Inc. Reproduced by permission.

"It's a real paradox," said Dr. Sharonne Hayes, director of the Mayo Clinic Women's Heart Clinic in Rochester, Minn. "Is it because women are still not getting aggressive enough care? . . . I think that's still part of it."

But even when men and women receive the same treatments, she said, studies have found women are more likely to develop complications after an intervention—and are still more likely to die. Now, researchers are beginning to investigate whether there are underlying physiological differences between men and women that could help explain not only why women fare worse, but also why diagnostic tests often miss their coronary artery disease.

"Cardiac disease in women has slightly different presentations, and the diagnostic tests may have different value than in men," said Dr. Nanette Wenger, professor of medicine in the division of cardiology at the Emory University School of Medicine in Atlanta. "The impact of risk factors may be different, but there may also be something else going on."

Searching for Explanations

The study of these gender-specific differences has become a promising area of investigation, drawing researchers who hope their insights will improve treatment —and increase women's survival rates.

One theory is that women, by virtue of being smaller, tend to have narrower vessels that may be more easily obstructed and more susceptible to damage from smoking, hypertension and diabetes. They may exhibit more diffuse blockages that elude diagnostic screens tested primarily on men.

Some clues may come from the relatively rare cases of young women, whose heart disease often is very aggressive. Generally, women are protected from heart disease until after menopause.

"If both a man and a woman have a heart attack at 50, the woman is going to have twice the rate of dying," Hayes said. No one knows why, but there are plenty of intriguing hypotheses. "Is the difference sex-based? Or is it genetic?" Hayes asked. "Women have more migraines—do they have more vascular spasms, squeezing and narrowing the arteries? Is the inflammatory component a stronger component in younger women? Are they more prone to blood clots because of their sex hormones?

"There's a lot of interest now at looking at those sex differences and seeing how we can use them to our advantage. . . . If clotting and inflammation are a problem, we have therapies that reduce clotting and inflammation."

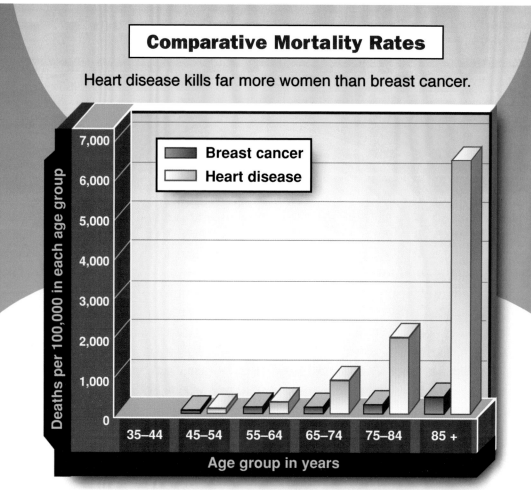

Comparative Mortality Rates

Heart disease kills far more women than breast cancer.

Legend:
- Breast cancer
- Heart disease

Y-axis: Deaths per 100,000 in each age group — 0, 1,000, 2,000, 3,000, 4,000, 5,000, 6,000, 7,000

X-axis: Age group in years — 35–44, 45–54, 55–64, 65–74, 75–84, 85 +

Taken from: Palo Alto Medical Foundation, "Menopause: Related Conditions." www.pamf.org/patients/menopauseconditions.html.

Right now, women are twice as likely as men to die from open-heart surgery. They're also more likely to suffer complications after procedures to open blocked arteries, especially bleeding complications, and they're more likely to suffer another cardiac event after the first.

They receive only a third of life-saving interventional procedures, such as balloon angioplasty and stenting, and a third of open-heart surgeries. And they're more likely than men to die within a year of a heart attack: 38 percent of women die, compared with 25 percent of men.

But many leading female cardiologists reject the notion that women suffer from biases in treatment. "There's a tendency in this field to jump to the conclusion that we're not doing right by our female patients," said Dr. Alexandra J. Lansky, director of the Women's Cardiovascular Health Initiative at the Cardiovascular Research Foundation in Manhattan. "That's not necessarily the case."

> **FAST FACT**
>
> Heart disease is not only the leading cause of death among women, it is also a leading cause of disability. Two-thirds of women who have a heart attack fail to make a full recovery.

Early Efforts Needed

But doctors are being encouraged to treat women more aggressively, Lansky said, because they benefit tremendously from interventional procedures using the new generation of drug-coated stents to open blocked arteries. "The results are beneficial, independent of vessel size," she said.

Women also display different patterns of blockage in their vessels. Men tend to have very discrete blockages at distinct focal points—making them more amenable to stenting, said Dr. Salvatore Trazzera, who runs a women's heart program that has offices in Huntington and Farmingdale [New York]. Women tend to have blockages that are more diffuse and that occupy a longer segment of the vessel, he said. These blockages still cause angina and chest pain, but their structure isn't amenable to interventions such as surgery and stenting, so they are treated with medications instead, Trazzera said.

Since women clearly fare worse than men once they have established heart disease, however, cardiologists say it is imperative they adapt preventive behaviors and a healthy lifestyle early in life. "We're trying to increase awareness in women at a much younger age, when they can actually prevent disease, rather than waiting until they're in their 60s—or even 40s and 50s," Trazzera said. "We're seeing a lot of older women who have heart disease. What were they doing in the 1960s and 1970s? They were smoking. And that becomes a factor later on in life—it has a lifelong effect on one's coronary status."

For reasons that are not well-understood, smoking is one of a number of risk factors that take more of a toll on women's coronary artery systems than on men's. A woman who smokes a half a pack of cigarettes a day, for example, has a higher chance of developing heart disease than a man who smokes the same amount, Hayes said.

High blood pressure also takes more of a toll on women, while levels of "good" and "bad" cholesterol may have different significance for men than for women.

Diabetics Fare Worst

Of all risk factors, however, it is diabetes that seems to have a dramatically more significant effect on women, multiplying their risk. The American Heart Association's new guidelines for diagnosing and treating heart disease in women, issued last week [in February 2005], specifically addressed this heightened risk, which has serious implications for black and Hispanic women because they have higher rates than white women of diabetes and hypertension, as well as heart disease.

"Diabetes is a double whammy for women," Hayes said, but it is not the only one. "If you made a list of risk factors, they'd be pretty much the same for men as for women. But how they affect men versus women does vary." Again, no one knows exactly why.

Making Women Aware

Part of the problem with disparate treatment outcomes may lie in the fact that women are still underrepresented in clinical trials to test devices and fine-tune procedures,

Model Helena Christensen on the runway at the Heart Truth Red Dress fashion show. The event is held to raise awareness of heart disease in women. **(AP Images.)**

despite a 1993 congressional mandate to include more women in research.

"We have to increase recruitment to clinical trials, where female representation is only 15 to 35 percent, at best," Lansky said. To understand if trial results involving new devices can be applied to both genders, she said, "we need more women in these trials."

Early stenting technology was bulkier than it is today; now, smaller catheters are available, and wire mesh stents come in different sizes, some much smaller than before. But women are often older than men when they develop heart disease, so they are more frail and more likely to have accompanying diseases that complicate treatment.

And women typically delay seeking medical attention when they are having a heart attack, often mistaking their chest pain for indigestion or heartburn. Their first symptoms are often unusual, such as inexplicable fatigue, lassitude or a decreased tolerance for physical activity.

Many younger women rely solely on a gynecologist for health care, and these physicians don't specialize in heart disease. They can, however, screen women and make referrals when necessary, experts say.

Technological Insights

Emerging technologies also hold the promise of better, more accurate results for women, said Dr. Jennifer Mieres, director of nuclear cardiology at North Shore University Hospital in Manhasset [New York]. "Women frequently come in with chest pain and may go to the catheterization lab and be told, 'It's all clear. It's psychological,'" Mieres said. "The women go home, and they still have chest pain and poor quality of life."

But now there's an explanation for the mysterious malaise. "Now we have data using cardiac MRIs [magnetic resonance images] that let us see the inner linings of the heart muscle, and we see that there is a problem,"

Mieres said. "The bottom line is that we're underestimating the burden of atherosclerosis in women with current technology."

Other emerging technologies include new, advanced, ultra-fast CT [computerized tomography] angiography for quick, non-invasive screening; intravascular ultrasound that may pick up atherosclerosis not detected otherwise, and the use of calcium scores as a marker for coronary artery disease.

Doctors say women must be proactive. Know your risk factors, and never postpone seeking medical attention for suspicious symptoms. Start with a healthy lifestyle: Don't smoke, lose weight, eat a heart-healthy diet and exercise regularly. And get screened so you know your individual risk factors.

"Know your numbers," Mieres said. "Know your cholesterol, know your blood sugar and pay attention to your family history. . . . You are vulnerable as well."

Even Young Athletes Are Vulnerable to Heart Attacks

Clinton Colmenares

Heart-attack victims are typically over thirty, but even young athletes can suffer a fatal attack under certain conditions. In the following selection Clinton Colmenares reports on the research of Fred Mueller, a University of North Carolina professor of exercise and sports science, who tracks the deaths of student athletes preparing for football season. According to Mueller, the problem comes when the core of the body overheats. This can place unmanageable stress on a person's heart. American football requires layers of protection for the players, and these act as insulation that traps heat within the body. Since football is a fall game, preparation normally begins in August, at the hottest time of the year. If the core of the body overheats or the brain malfunctions from overheating, the heart may give out. In 2006 Mueller recorded a dozen heat-related deaths among young football players. It was the highest total since the 1930s, when such records began to be kept. Clinton Colmenares is the editor for research news at the University of North Carolina at Chapel Hill. He was previously the national news director at Vanderbilt University Medical Center.

SOURCE: Clinton Colmenares, "Heat-Related Deaths in Middle, High School Football Players Spike in 2006," *University of North Carolina News*, August 2, 2007. Reproduced by permission.

Every year, Fred Mueller, professor of exercise and sports science at the University of North Carolina at Chapel Hill, compiles a sports list, but unlike popular pre-season picks or a glamorous hot-recruit sheet, nobody envies him this task. Some years the list is longer than others, but, Mueller said, there's no reason any kid should be on it.

It's a list of boys who died playing or practicing football, kids whose body temperatures rose so high and so fast under the summer sun that their brains couldn't keep up, couldn't regulate their cores, and the boys died. "When something is preventable. . . ," Mueller said, shaking his head. "Those kids could be alive today."

Five young athletes, from 11 to 17 years old, died of heat stroke in 2006. The trend was declining. The last time there were more than five was 1972, when there were seven. In five of the past 16 years there were none. But, Mueller said, there have been 31 since 1995, and all of them could have been avoided.

Seven other players died last year [2006] of "heart-related" deaths that might or might not have been related to heat or exertion. "And we don't know the number of kids who had heat exhaustion," said Mueller, in UNC's College of Arts & Sciences.

Steps for Prevention

With summer practice about to swing into high gear, Mueller said it's time to remember these kids, and to keep in mind how heat-related deaths can be prevented.

- Require each athlete to have a physical and know if an athlete has a history of heat-related illness; these kids are more susceptible to heat stroke. Overweight players are also at higher risk.

- Acclimatize players to the heat slowly; North Carolina mandates that the first three days of practice be done without uniforms.

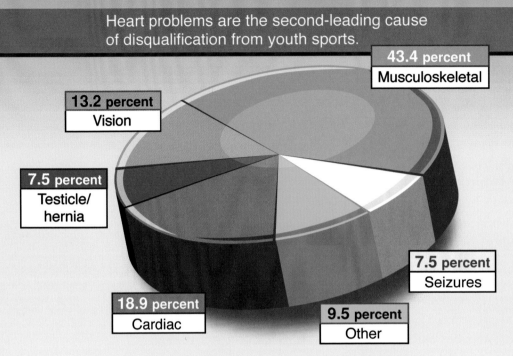

A Commonplace Threat to Boys

Heart problems are the second-leading cause of disqualification from youth sports.

43.4 percent
Musculoskeletal

13.2 percent
Vision

7.5 percent
Testicle/ hernia

7.5 percent
Seizures

18.9 percent
Cardiac

9.5 percent
Other

Taken from: Jay Smith and Edward R. Laskowski, "The Preparticipation Physical Examination: Mayo Clinic Experience with 2,739 Examinations," *Mayo Clinic Proceedings*, No. 73, 1998, pp. 419–29.

- Alter practice schedules to avoid long workouts in high-humidity.
- Provide cold water before, during and after practice in unlimited quantities.
- Provide shaded rest areas with circulating air; remove helmets and loosen or remove jerseys; some schools have plastic outdoor pools filled with ice for cool-downs after practice.
- Know the symptoms of heat illness: nausea, incoherence, fatigue, weakness, vomiting, muscle cramps, weak rapid pulse, visual disturbance. Contrary to popular belief, heat stroke victims may sweat profusely.

• Have an emergency plan in place; parents should inquire about emergency plans for their kids' teams.

Heat Kills

Heat-related deaths are compiled as part of the Annual Survey of Football Injuries, research that began in 1931; Mueller took the reins in 1980. The survey tracks major injuries and deaths in 1.8 million football players from sandlot (organized, non-school affiliated teams), middle school, high school, college and professional teams.

There were a total of 20 deaths in 2006; two sandlot players, three in college, 13 middle and high schoolers.

High school junior Kale Prothero takes a drink of water during football practice. Heat stroke can be a danger for football players and can even cause death in young athletes. **(AP Images.)**

Only one death was directly related to the game: a 17-year-old high school player who received a spinal cord injury when tackled in a practice drill. Rules against "spearing," or leading blocks and tackles with the helmet or face mask, have drastically reduced the number of direct injuries, Mueller said.

The heat-related injuries warrant special attention because they are preventable, he said. These and other "indirect" deaths and injuries were the highest since 1936, when there were 18. Mueller said there still exists a hard-core mentality in some football circles, where kids feel pressured from coaches or parents not to complain about feeling ill during practices or games.

But machismo doesn't affect physiology. Physical activity raises players' temperatures higher than normal, Mueller said. When body temperatures rise to 103 or 104, the brain's hypothalamus loses its ability to regulate the heat. The heart beats faster to increase blood flow to the skin to aid in evaporation, leaving less blood in the heart and other muscles. Brain death begins around 106 degrees, but death from heat stroke can be gradual, taking three or four days while organs begin to fail.

"Coaches, athletes and parents should be aware that all fall sports could lead to heat-related deaths if precautions aren't taken," Mueller said. "Every year we have to get the word out."

And every year, he has to make a list.

> **FAST FACT**
>
> During heatstroke, it is not the peak degree of internal temperature elevation that is key to survival, but rather limiting the length of time that the body temperature is elevated above a critical level of 106°F.

Mammography May Prove Useful in Detecting Heart Disease

Jonathan R. Adkins et al.

A common but hard-to-spot cause of heart attacks is blockage of the arteries that supply oxygen to the heart. If detected, the problem can be prevented through bypass surgery, in which a new artery is put in place of the one that has been clogged with calcium. In the following selection a group of surgeons, led by Jonathan R. Adkins, report on their study of the use of mammography to detect the need for bypass surgery to protect the heart. They report that women who have an annual X-ray exam of their breasts can benefit by having the same exam look for calcium buildups in their arteries. Although the study was small, the authors state that their findings are significant and should prompt further investigation. Adkins is a clinical postdoctoral fellow at the Baylor College of Medicine. His five coauthors are also surgeons.

SOURCE: Jonathan Adkins et al., "Mammography as Screening for Coronary Artery Disease," *American Surgeon*, vol. 73, July 2007, pp. 717–20. Copyright © 2007, Southeastern Surgical Congress. Reproduced by permission.

oronary heart disease is the leading cause of death in American women. More than 250,000 women sustain a myocardial infarction [heart attack] annually. Perhaps because of breast cancer awareness, women still perceive breast cancer as a greater risk than coronary heart disease, even though women diagnosed with coronary heart disease experience greater morbidity and mortality than men. This may lead women to underestimate their risk for coronary artery disease (CAD) and fail to seek early interventions to prevent unnecessary morbidity and mortality.

Screening mammograms for the early detection of breast cancer are recommended for women starting at age

Coronary Artery Calcification by Sex and Age

The buildup of calcium in the arteries that feed the heart rises steeply with age, especially in men.

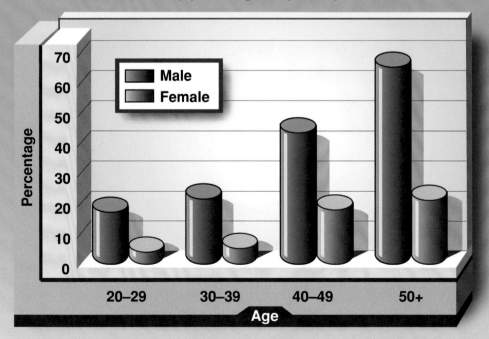

Taken from: Bill Sardi, "Who Will Tell the People? It Isn't Cholesterol!" *Knowledge of Health*, January 31, 2007.

40, and it is estimated that 75 per cent of women in the United States follow this recommendation, resulting in more than 50 million mammograms performed annually. Recent studies have shown that breast arterial calcifications (BAC) identified on routine screening mammography in otherwise healthy women older than 50 are associated with an increased cardiovascular morbidity and mortality. This association between heart disease and BAC has not been extensively studied. Currently, radiologists do not consistently include BAC in their reports, and BAC seen on screening mammography is thought to be of no clinical significance. The purpose of this study is to determine further the relationship between mammographically detected BAC and CAD disease.

Scoring Arteries

After appropriate institutional review board approval, we retrospectively identified women undergoing coronary artery bypass grafting (CABG) at our institution over a 5-year period (1997–2001). From this group of women with CAD, we reviewed their records to determine those women who had also undergone mammographic screening in our institution. The mammograms from this group of women were reviewed by our dedicated mammographers for the presence of BAC. Because no system of grading BAC exists, we devised a method to categorize the degree of BAC into mild, moderate, and severe. We also attempted to quantify the severity of the CAD by the number of vessels requiring bypass. Other variables such as diabetes, hypertension, cholesterol, and obesity were also recorded and evaluated according to significance. Our review identified 44 women who underwent CABG and screening mammography in our institution. Of these women, 18 of 44 (41%) had BAC identified on their screening mammograms. . . .

The prevalence of BAC in coronary artery bypass patients was significantly greater than that seen in the general population reported in previous studies. Based on our severity scores, we identified 10 women with mild, three with moderate, and five with severe BAC on mammography. The degree of BAC did not correlate with the number of vessels requiring bypass. Of the 18 women with BAC, seven (38.8%) had diabetes, 16 (88.8%) had hypertension, 11 (61.1%) were overweight (body mass index > 25), and 10 (55.5%) had hypercholesterolemia [high cholesterol].

Risks Vary

Cardiovascular disease is the leading cause of morbidity and mortality in the United States and other industrialized countries. For many asymptomatic individuals, the first manifestation of underlying disease is often an unexpected acute myocardial infarction or sudden death. Risk factors such as smoking, dyslipidemia [an intolerance of fatty acids], hypertension, and obesity have been unable to identify a great number of patients at risk for a fatal cardiac event. More than 60 per cent of all cardiac events are experienced by individuals thought to be at low to intermediate risk, which includes 75 per cent of the population. This has resulted in considerable interest in new methods that would allow for early detection of individuals at increased risk for these events.

Modern mammographic equipment is designed specifically for the detection of microcalcifications.

Several imaging techniques have been used to identify atherosclerosis. Ultrasound, MRI [magnetic resonance imaging], and CT [computerized tomography] have shown the ability to predict patients with vascular disease. However, these tests are not practical screening tools because of the extra cost and lack of proven superi-

FAST FACT

A study of 10,377 men, published in 2003, found that calcium accumulations in the coronary arteries were strongly associated with the risk of heart attack, independent of other risk factors.

ority when compared with traditional risk assessment. There is also considerable radiation exposure to women undergoing yearly CT scans. Because cardiovascular disease and breast cancer are the leading causes of death in women older than the age of 50, mammography, used as a dual diagnostic tool, could represent a very cost-effective strategy.

Common Test

Mammography is recommended annually for women age 40 and older as a breast cancer screening tool coupled with a yearly physical exam. An added benefit of this routine screening tool would be to detect BAC as a possible sign of CAD. Identification of BAC on mammograms is not difficult, and developing a grading scale

A doctor reviews mammogram results with his patient. Mammography may help detect heart disease. (© Lara Jo Regan/Liaison/Getty Images.)

could be easily established. The grading scale we used is subjective but consistent, because the same individuals reviewed each mammogram. Mammograms with arterial calcifications that were barely visible and few in number were labeled mild. If the calcifications were easily visible and present throughout the breast, then we labeled it severe. Anything in between these two was labeled moderate. . . .

Although other studies have looked at the association between BAC and risk factors for vascular disease, or the presence of vascular disease seen on diagnostic studies, none have studied the direct correlation between patients with known CAD requiring revascularization, [bypass] and BAC. Our study suggests that women with BAC found on their screening mammogram may benefit from further evaluation for CAD. The women that would benefit most from this appear to be those who are thought to be low to intermediate risk for CAD and found to have BAC on screening mammogram. Perhaps these women should undergo further workup for CAD, with the potential benefit of early intervention.

Our pilot study is limited by the number of patients reported, but represents important findings on which to base further evaluation.

Fish Oil Shows Promise in Preventing Heart Disease

Sabrina Rubin Erdely, Denny Watkins, and Katy Gagnon

The benefits of natural supplements are a matter of hot debate in medical circles. Fish oil, or more specifically the omega-3 fatty acids it contains, is highly praised for its health benefits, especially to the heart. In the following selection three journalists present the case for the virtues of fish oil. In particular, they cite cardiologists who believe that omega-3s protect the heart by reducing inflammation in the arteries. However, not all medical professionals agree about the health benefits of fish oil. The authors pointedly note that the active compounds in fish oil have been left off the federal government's list of daily recommended nutrients. Sabrina Rubin Erdely is a journalist who has written for *Philadelphia Magazine* and other publications. Denny Watkins is an award-nominated researcher for *Men's Health* magazine. As a student at the University of Oregon, Katy Gagnon won a national award for in-depth journalism.

SOURCE: Sabrina Rubin Erdely, Denny Watkins, and Katy Gagnon, "The Government's Big Fish Story," *Men's Health*, vol. 22, July/August 2007, pp. 154–60. Copyright © 2007 Rodale, Inc. Reproduced by permission.

When Randal McCloy was rushed to West Virginia University Ruby Memorial Hospital's intensive-care unit, he was practically dead. The 27-year-old coal miner had spent 41 hours buried 2 1/2 miles underground after an explosion in the Sago, West Virginia, mine where he'd been working. His 12 oxygen-starved colleagues had all perished.

"As far as we know, he survived the longest exposure to carbon monoxide poisoning," says Julian Bailes, M.D., the neurosurgeon assigned to the case. McCloy was in a coma and in deep shock, his heart barely beating, one of his lungs collapsed, his liver and both kidneys shut down. Even if he somehow managed to pull through, doctors predicted McCloy would be severely brain damaged, since the carbon monoxide had stripped the protective myelin sheath from most of his brain's neurons. "It's very difficult to come back from a brain injury," says Dr. Bailes. "There's no drug that can help that."

While McCloy was being given oxygen infusions in a hyperbaric chamber, Dr. Bailes was struck by inspiration: He ordered a daily dose of 15,000 milligrams (mg) docosahexaenoic acid (DHA) and eicosapentaenoic acid (EPA) for the miner. In layman's terms? "Fish oil," says Dr. Bailes.

Several weeks passed. Then, unexpectedly, McCloy emerged from his coma. This in itself was amazing, but he wasn't done. In the weeks that followed, he stunned even the most optimistic experts by recovering his memory and gradually regaining his ability to walk, talk, and see, a turnaround that many in the medical field called miraculous.

Although Dr. Bailes believes the hyperbaric chamber may have worked some magic on the myelin, he thinks much of the credit belongs elsewhere. "The omega-3s helped rebuild the damaged gray and white matter of his brain," says Dr. Bailes, who now takes his own medicine, swallowing a fish-oil supplement each morning.

On his orders, McCloy, still recuperating at home, continues to take fish oil daily. "I would say he should be on it for a lifetime," says Dr. Bailes. "But then, I think everybody should."

Maybe what fish oil needed all along was a better publicist. After all, this isn't the medical community's first infatuation with omega-3s. Back in 1970, a pair of Danish researchers, Hans Olaf Bang and Jørn Dyerberg, traveled to Greenland to uncover why the Eskimo population there had a low incidence of heart disease despite subsisting on a high-fat diet. Their finding: The Eskimos' blood contained high levels of omega-3s, establishing the first link to heart health. But even though this discovery spurred additional omega-3 research throughout the '70s and '80s, the public remained more interested in other nutrients—none of which had the unfortunate words "fish" or "fatty" in their names.

There are three types of omega-3s: DHA and EPA, found in fish and marine algae (which is where the fish get them), and alpha-linolenic acid (ALA), which is found in plants, seeds, and nuts. All three have health benefits, but those attributed to DHA and EPA have sparked renewed interest in recent years. Studies show that this tag team may not only reduce a person's risk of heart disease and stroke but also possibly help prevent ailments as diverse as arthritis, Alzheimer's disease, asthma, autoimmune disorders, and attention-deficit/ hyperactivity disorder—and those are just the As. Researchers are now exploring if these multifunctional fats can, among other things, ward off cancer and even make prison inmates less violent. It's enough to make omega-3 geeks downright giddy.

"Omega-3s are fantastic!" says Jing X. Kang, M.D., Ph.D., a Harvard University researcher who made the news by genetically engineering pigs to produce omega-3s in their meat. "Not just for your heart but also for brain function, immunity function, women's health, children's health—I'm amazed at how important they are."

Controversial Claims

In fact, some experts argue that omega-3s should be labeled essential nutrients as necessary to health as, say, vitamins A and D. "They're involved in the metabolism of each individual cell," says Artemis P. Simopoulos, M.D., a physician and the president of the Center for Genetics, Nutrition and Health in Washington, D.C. "They're part of your body's basic nutrition."

But while some see omega-3s as a nutritional no-brainer, others find them surprisingly controversial. "Omega-3s are way, way overhyped," says Marion Nestle, Ph.D., M.P.H., a professor of nutrition and public health at New York University and the author of *What to Eat*. "The research so far has been mixed. I'll grant that they're healthy, but I don't think if you don't eat them you're going to die of a heart attack."

The government has been equally cautious. So far, the Food and Drug Administration [FDA] has issued only a tepid statement that "supportive but not conclusive research" indicates that DHA and EPA are good for your heart. And the Food and Nutrition Board—the scientific panel that, funded mostly by federal money, creates Daily Recommended Intakes (DRI) for essential nutrients—has shrugged off the issue altogether. It crowned ALA essential, but ignored DHA and EPA. "We didn't feel the data were sufficient," says Linda Meyers, Ph.D., director of the board. It's precisely the sort of comment that leaves omega-3 researchers flabbergasted.

"They're in the Dark Ages," says Bill Lands, Ph.D., a retired National Institutes of Health (NIH) biochemist who has written extensively about omega-3s and is widely considered the field's elder statesman. "The science was very clear 15 years ago. But they're not interested in science. All they're interested in doing is preserving the status quo, when they could be saving lives.". . .

> **FAST FACT**
>
> The American Heart Association recommends eating fish—especially fatty fish—at least twice a week as a source of omega-3 fatty acids.

Not Enough Fish Consumed

The average American ate only 16.2 pounds of fish in 2005, but consumed 195 pounds of meat. And although our livers can manufacture tiny amounts of DHA and EPA when we eat lots of ALA-rich nuts and seeds, these aren't exactly our favorite foods, either.

Changing agricultural techniques have worsened the situation. The natural omega-3 contents of meat, milk, and eggs have plummeted now that our livestock no longer graze on ALA-rich grass, instead consuming corn, wheat, and other grains that are loaded with another group of fatty acids, called omega-6s. In fact, the disappearance of omega-3s from our diets has coincided with an upsurge in omega-6s, mainly in the form of cereals, grains, and processed foods made with hydrogenated

Omega-3 Content of Popular Meats and Seafood

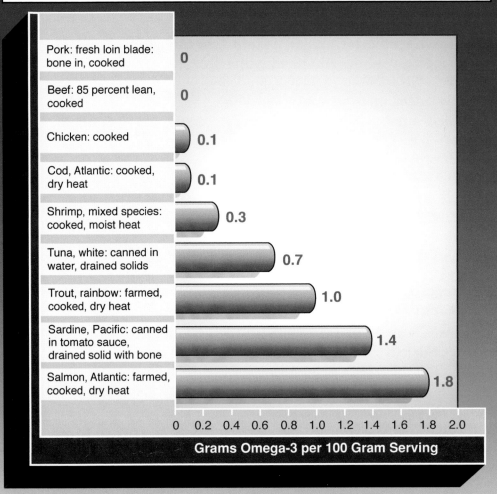

Pork: fresh loin blade: bone in, cooked	0
Beef: 85 percent lean, cooked	0
Chicken: cooked	0.1
Cod, Atlantic: cooked, dry heat	0.1
Shrimp, mixed species: cooked, moist heat	0.3
Tuna, white: canned in water, drained solids	0.7
Trout, rainbow: farmed, cooked, dry heat	1.0
Sardine, Pacific: canned in tomato sauce, drained solid with bone	1.4
Salmon, Atlantic: farmed, cooked, dry heat	1.8

Grams Omega-3 per 100 Gram Serving

Taken from: USDA Nutrient Database for Standard Reference.

oils. Dr. Simopoulos estimates that in caveman days, we ate an equal amount of the two types, but that the average American now eats 16 times more omega-6s than omega-3s. . . .

Omega-3s act as a sort of internal ice pack, in part because they spur our bodies to produce several inflammation-lowering substances. "Omega-3s work along the same biochemical pathway as a COX-2 inhibitor, such as Vioxx, but farther upstream," says Dr. Meade, meaning that omega-3s treat the underlying problem rather than the symptoms. And emerging research indicates that this powerful ability to ease inflammation is one of the ways omega-3s may help prevent a number of ailments, including . . . heart attack and stroke.

Good for the Heart

Cardiologists now believe that chronic inflammation triggers the release of artery-blocking plaque. In the most definitive study to date, published in the *Lancet*, heart-attack survivors who took 900 mg fish oil daily were 30 percent less likely to die of a second heart attack, and 20 percent less likely to suffer a stroke, than those who skipped the supplement.

Omega-3s can guard your arteries in other ways, too, since they also lower triglycerides and make blood vessels more elastic. Add in their ability to improve electrical communication between cardiac cells, thereby preventing arrhythmia, and you can see why omega-3s are a standard part of cardiac care in Europe. If you have a heart attack in Italy, France, Britain, or Spain, the hospital will even send you home with a prescription for Omacor, a "medication" that's super-purified DHA and EPA.

Left Off List

In the world of nutrition, few events make a scientist's palms sweat as much as the release of a newly revised DRI list. Before the Food and Nutrition Board announced its most recent DRI for fatty acids, in 2002, some experts were optimistic that omega-3s would make the cut, given the research strides made over the previous decade. Instead, DHA and EPA were nowhere to be found—snubbed yet again by the larger scientific community. Even worse, the new DRI recommended that adults continue eating 10 times as many omega-6s as omega-3s, a ratio that practically gave omega-3 researchers a heart attack.

But Alice Lichtenstein, D.Sc., a Tufts University public-health professor who was on the panel that voted DHA down, doesn't see what all the fuss is about. "There just wasn't enough data to go on," she says. "What's out there is a little difficult to interpret."

Part of the problem she's referring to is that some studies didn't account for the amount of omega-6s that research participants consumed (too much blunts the effects of omega-3s), and other supplement studies didn't adjust for how much fish their participants ate. The differences make the studies hard to compare.

"It's all over the place," says Sharon Akabas, Ph.D., codirector of the master's program at Columbia University's institute of human nutrition, which held a symposium on this very problem. "It's like dealing with a moving target." Also, since most omega-3 research has focused on curing the sick, no one has yet pinned down how much DHA and EPA keeps healthy people well. Without that magic number, the Food and Nutrition Board says, its hands are tied.

The board's cautious approach is typical of how slow our government is to accept scientific change, say advocates of omega-3s. For example, although the World Health Organization endorsed adding DHA to infant formula back in 1994, it took the FDA until 2002 to approve the move. "Fifty-nine countries added DHA to infant formula before we did," says Dr. Simopoulos. "Mexico and China were ahead of us! And that's because our government is 20 years behind when it comes to the science."

Nevertheless, Meyers insists that the Food and Nutrition Board is just being thorough. "Anything in nutrition is going to lead to controversy," she says. "No matter the issue, some people will say we don't go far enough and others will say we go too far."

Perhaps, but it's revealing that even though important studies have come out since the board's 2002 list, it has no plans to revisit the status of DHA, despite the fact that at least one panelist has changed her mind. "There's a growing consensus that we should be eating more DHA for sure, as well as EPA," says Penny Kris-Etherton, Ph.D., a Penn State University professor of nutrition. "I would like to see stronger dietary recommendations than we currently have."

Lifestyle Changes Can Help Head Off a Heart Attack

Lynnell Nixon-Knight

Heart disease is complicated to treat, but the path to prevention is relatively straightforward. In the following selection author Lynnell Nixon-Knight describes both the innovative treatments and the simple methods of heart-disease prevention that doctors are recommending. Lifestyle change is the key to prevention, she writes. That comes down, essentially, to eating right and getting enough exercise. Making a positive change in lifestyle can actually reverse some of the damage caused by overeating and inactivity, she reports. Nixon-Knight is an Indiana-based journalist who writes on medical topics for the Indiana University School of Medicine, among others.

The latest findings on heart health come with good news and bad news. The bad news is: Heart disease is currently more common in the U.S. than all cancers combined. The good news is: Everyone can do something to improve their cardiac health. . . .

SOURCE: Lynnell Nixon-Knight, "Heart Matters," *Indianapolis Monthly Medical Guide*, 2007, pp. 9–14. Reproduced by permission.

"From a medical economics position, it's frightening to think where we're going to be in 10 years," says Gregory Elsner MD, an interventional cardiologist affiliated with The Heart Center of Indiana. "As a state we may work hard, but we don't exercise. Our long hours often lead to lots of fast food and a low activity level."

Though fighting heart disease is a burning issue for public health policymakers, it's a far less protracted battle for individual people. By making a few simple lifestyle changes, a person's risk for heart disease can be lessened almost immediately. But a few common hurdles have to be overcome first.

Hunger is a hard driver for nearly everyone. When someone cuts their food intake, their stomach may be prone to sound the alarm between meals. Elsner doesn't advise against snacking, rather he puts emphasis on the type of snacking people should do. "If you're hungry, eat a little something, but choose an item that's healthy," he says. "Instead of grabbing a candy bar, grab a piece of fruit or some cut-up vegetables."

Obesity can be fought via surgery and drugs as well as diet and exercise, but lifestyle change is the easiest—and cheapest—method for most. Those who struggle with extreme obesity may benefit from bariatric surgery, which physically limits one's food intake by either restricting the size of the stomach or by re-routing the digestive tract to reduce calorie absorption. The procedure is effective, but it's a step reserved for severe cases, says Elsner. Many people dream of the day when a simple once-a-day pill will cure obesity, but most existing appetite-suppressant drugs have had potential side effects or have proven ineffective. "Most over-the-counter weight-loss drugs are amphetamine-based products," says Elsner. "Many are stimulants, which can have

> **FAST FACT**
>
> The four main lifestyle changes that reduce the risk of coronary artery disease are quitting smoking, maintaining a healthy diet, exercising, and reducing stress.

undesirable side effects." One example is the drug "fen-phen," a combination of the drugs fenfluramine and phentermine, which suppresses appetite but also can harm the heart—a poor tradeoff overall.

Blocking the Urge

One drug in development, however, appears to be an effective appetite suppressant without an accompanying stimulant. "This new drug actually blocks the same receptor that marijuana affects, the endo cannabinoid receptor," says Elsner. "It's also helped for smoking cessation as well—another huge risk factor for heart disease." Although this drug has been approved in Europe, it has not yet been approved by the Food and Drug Administration for use in the United States.

As close as this seems to a magic pill, there is still a need to do the hard work of eating well. "Our Western diet is very unhealthy," says Robert J. Robison MD, chairman of cardiovascular surgery at St. Vincent Hospitals and managing partner of the cardiothoracic division of CorVasc MDs. "Eating a normal Western diet is almost like poisoning yourself." He especially disparages most fast-food fare, which is all-too-often the quick dinner fix of choice for many American families. "There are healthy items even on those menus—you really should train yourself to select those. Instead, we usually pick a nice big piece of beef with French fries," he says. "You might as well pour them right into your coronary arteries, because that's where they're going."

On the whole, keeping an eye on one's food intake is part of a healthy lifestyle that needs to begin in childhood years. Calcium buildup in arteries, a harbinger of heart disease, has been found in people in their 20s, and even in teenagers. Atherosclerosis (the condition where fatty plaque forms on the inside of arterial linings) and heart failure, once seen almost exclusively in older adults, is creeping down into middle-aged Americans

Rising Childhood Obesity

The threat to heart health begins with childhood obesity.

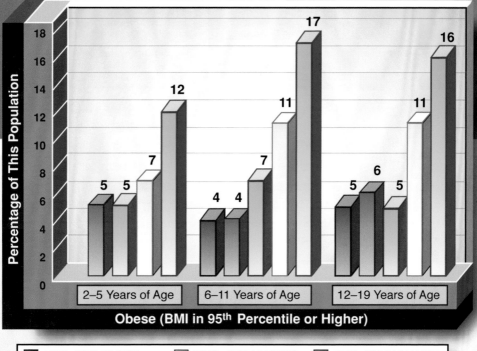

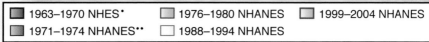

Obese (BMI in 95th Percentile or Higher)

- 1963–1970 NHES*
- 1971–1974 NHANES**
- 1976–1980 NHANES
- 1988–1994 NHANES
- 1999–2004 NHANES

*NHES: National Health Examination Survey
**NHANES: National Health and Nutrition Examination Survey

Taken from: Robert Wood Johnson Foundation, "Childhood Obesity," 2006 Annual Report.
www.rwif.org/files/publications/annual/2006/yir/childhood-obesity.html.

as poor diet and exercise become pandemic across the culture.

Along with its other many negative outcomes, smoking is a giant risk factor for heart disease, damaging the blood vessels in a number of ways. "There are irritants in tobacco that cause inflammation in the bloodstream and can make the blood more sticky and gooey, causing it to stick to the vessel wall and make the arteries spasm," says Woodrow Corey MD, FACC, director of cardiology and interventional cardiology at Clarian North Medical

Center. "There are a lot of nasty ingredients that get into your blood from a cigarette—I'd say smoking is probably the worst thing you can do for your heart."

Risk of Obesity

Diabetes is also a very high risk factor for heart disease and stroke, as well as a host of other related problems. The condition begins with men and women who settle into sedentary habits as they age, eventually gaining fat pounds they can't lose easily. The weight gain gets worse until they develop metabolic syndrome, a group of risk factors for coronary disease, and people who have metabolic syndrome are at an increased risk for type-II diabetes. Some of the risk factors included in metabolic syndrome are abdominal obesity, high blood pressure, high cholesterol and insulin resistance.

Even if someone has none of these conditions, they may not realize when they should begin receiving an annual cardiovascular checkup. "Well, sometimes middle-aged people who've been inactive may want to start an exercise regimen, and that would be a good time to get the heart checked," says Corey. "There are obviously different categories of risk, but I would suggest a routine evaluation at age 40."

Corey suggests getting a good over-all physical examination, a stress test to measure how one's blood pressure reacts under exercise, and an electrocardiogram (EKG), which graphs the electrical variations in the heart during activity or exercise. Abnormalities on an EKG might indicate a blocked artery somewhere. "This would also be a good time to do a lipid profile in addition to a cholesterol check," he says. "A lot of times people only do a 'total cholesterol' check, but a lipid panel looks at different subsections."

One element of a cholesterol check measures triglycerides, the chemical form that most fat takes in the body: overproduction leads to obesity. The body manufactures this fat from excessive calories that are not burned up at the end of the day. "Everyone has a basic metabolic rate (BMR)," explains Corey. "We will burn a certain number of calories just by being alive and doing basic functions." The BMR varies from person to person, based on size, sex, age and activity level; for the average person, the BMR should roughly match the daily calorie intake.

"Say your BMR is 2,000 calories—that's how many calories you would burn up in 24 hours doing your daily activities—and you eat 2,000 calories so you'd have zero left over, no gain or loss," says Corey. "Then say you pig out the next day and eat 3,000 calories. That extra thousand you didn't use gets stored in a little bank, and just sits there. If you do the same thing for two or three more days until you have a total of 3,500 extra calories, then you've just earned an extra pound."

The good news is that the organic balance sheet works the other way as well. To lose weight you must eat fewer calories or increase the BMR with activity. The thing to remember is that it takes as long to lose it as it does to gain it. (It just always seems longer.)

Aerobic exercise is good for strengthening the heart, and just needs to be maintained for 30 minutes to be effective. But you can get too much of a good thing. "If you're not in good shape and don't build up to that level of exercise, you can over-shoot your heart rate," Corey adds. "If that happens, it's using up too much oxygen and that could be dangerous. Also, there might be some undetected blockages in the blood vessels. At a lower rate the heart is not demanding much oxygen, but if you 'push the gas pedal' and rev the heart, it won't be able to get enough oxygen and you can develop an arrhythmia [an irregular heart beat] or even go into cardiac arrest."

Aspirin Can Help

In general, aspirin therapy to thin the blood is recommended for men starting around age 50; its effectiveness in women is still under study. Coronary blockages are sometimes due to inflammation, and aspirin can help to reduce that as well. Before taking aspirin, however, patients need to make sure they're not at risk for bleeding or have other risks associated with the medication, and therefore should see a doctor first. (In fact, people should consult a physician before beginning any new medical regimen, whether it involves medication or exercise.)

Once coronary-artery disease is established, there are three branches of treatment. One is through pharmaceu-

Tom Burns pauses during a jog to tie his shoe. Burns decided to change his lifestyle after both his father and grandfather died young from heart disease. (**AP Images.**)

ticals, although this route is usually reserved for patients with either the mildest forms of the disease, or patients who are not candidates for other treatments. For example, statins (cholesterol-lowering drugs) may be prescribed if cholesterol levels are high, or as a preventative measure if a patient has a family history of heart disease. "There are certainly advantages to the pharmaceutical approach, but it is also limited in what it can accomplish," says John Paris MD, a cardiac surgeon with Cor-Vasc MDs. "It does not prolong the patient's life, but it does help with the symptoms."

Angioplasties and other treatments involving stents and catheters are a second and more invasive type of treatment. By inserting flexible tubes into the body through small incisions, doctors can perform balloon angioplasties (which literally use a balloon to widen blood vessels) and stenting (the use of a slender wire tube to keep the blood vessels open) to relieve blockage in blood vessels. This type of procedure is easier for patients than full-blown operations, but the results may not last. "Some newer studies show stents don't last as long as hoped—even the newer drug-eluting stents," says Paris.

The most invasive treatment for heart disease is coronary bypass grafting surgery, in which blood vessels from other body sites are transplanted to the heart, providing a "bypass" around arteries that have been narrowed by fat, cholesterol and/or scar tissue. The treatment's obvious disadvantages include its complexity—it's a big operation that results in a long recovery time for the patient, as well as a certain amount of risk. "Surgery does provide the most durable results of any treatment for coronary disease," says Paris. . . .

Silent Threat

Part of the challenge of diagnosing heart disease stems from its occasional lack of symptoms—especially in women. "The symptoms women have tend to be atypical or unusual with what we usually associate with the heart," says George E. Revtyak MD, an interventional cardiologist with Methodist Cardiology.

Hormones generated by the ovaries protect against plaque buildup to a degree, and in the past, premenopausal women had a much lower incidence of heart problems. However, changes in lifestyles have lessened that protection, and today statistics show a pretty even split between men and women suffering from heart disease. . . .

Reducing the Risk

What's worse: When coronary artery disease is manifested clinically in women, it is usually more severe and less responsive to therapies such as stent replacement and bypass therapy. When applied to women, routine therapies have a higher mortality rate and poorer long-term results.

Fortunately, there is a way to reduce one's risk for heart disease, and it doesn't involve expensive medicine. "This may sound trite, but it simply comes down to diet and exercise," says Revtyak. Eat less and exercise more—moderation is the key. He also stresses that proper lifestyle choices can make up for some lost ground and adds, "If you haven't had a heart attack, you can reverse some, if not all, of the chemical imbalances that increase your risk. The important message here is that it's never too late to start living healthy."

The other key to beating heart disease is early diagnosis and treatment. Symptoms can be iffy—some surgeons claim that as many as 50 percent of their operative patients had no classic symptoms—so it's crucial to have checkups on a regular basis, especially if patients are diabetic, have a family history of heart disease or any of its associated risk factors.

One area man who was a non-smoker, maintained a slim weight with a good diet, and ran over five miles five times a week nearly died from a massive heart attack at age 44. Despite his relatively young age and a complete lack of symptoms, his condition required triple bypass surgery. "I was shocked because I thought I was doing everything right," he says. "As it turns out, the doctor told me my body is literally a 'cholesterol-making machine,' and if I hadn't been living the way I do, I would've probably died 10 years ago."

Paris admits that those prone to heart disease may not be able to prevent it entirely, but not doing anything can make it a lot worse a lot faster. "Riverview has a 'Get Heart Smart' program, and following those guidelines can, at a bare minimum, delay development of the disease," he says. "And who knows, maybe during the time of delay, someone's going to come up with the next breakthrough."

CHAPTER 2

Controversies About Heart Disease

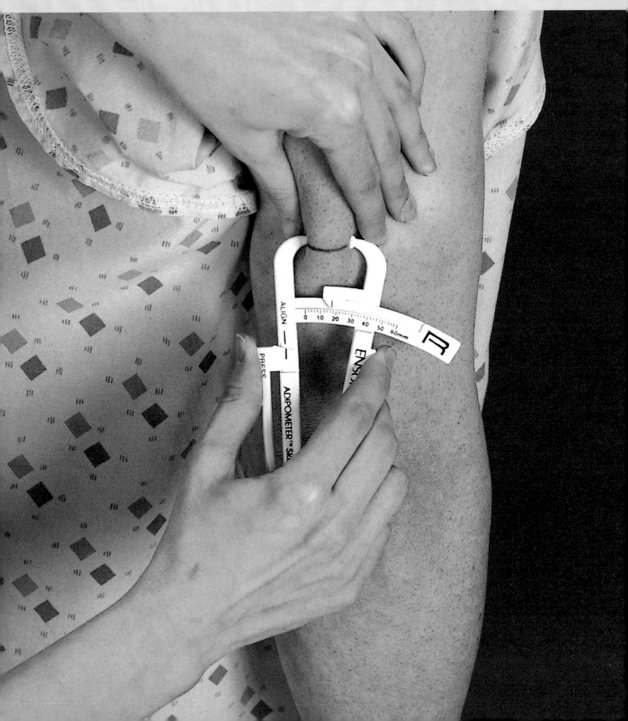

Body Fat Is a Threat to the Heart

Mary Desaulniers

The cultural acceptability of fat has varied widely throughout history. In the following selection health consultant Mary Desaulniers takes account of the irony that at a time when thin is in, so many Americans are becoming obese. The problem with being grossly overweight is not cultural, however, but medical. Obesity, she points out, is associated with high levels of heart-threatening low-density cholesterol, which can form a waxy buildup in arteries, and triglycerides, which are fatty molecules that circulate in the blood. Obese people tend to be less active, which in itself could lead to health problems, but according to Desaulniers excess fat itself has been shown in studies to lead to increased risk of heart disease. As fat-induced malfunctions pile up, the immune system itself can begin to cause problems for the heart. Rather than let that happen, she advocates taking whatever steps necessary to combat obesity. Former teacher Desaulniers is a lifestyle and weight management consultant. She has hosted an Internet radio show called *Reclaiming the Body's Wisdom*.

Photo on facing page. This triceps-skinfold test measures the ratio of fat to body mass. Some argue that obesity raises the risk of heart disease. **(From Fundamentals of Nursing, Standards and Practices, 2nd edition by Delaune/Ladner, © 2002. Reprinted with permission of Delmar Learning.)**

We only have to look at a [sixteenth-century Italian painter] Titian painting to recognize that at one point in the history of Western culture, fat was considered beautiful. Before the 20th century, corpulence was touted as a sign of wealth and luxury, largely because most people were barely surviving on a meager existence.

Ironically, now in our era of affluence and plenty, we have to contend with the health and economic problems of obesity. We have a population in North America that is more than 55% overweight. More than 20% of those overweight are considered obese, a situation which proves to be an economic burden on our health care system because of the coronary risk factors associated with obesity. In 2004, total national health expenditure in the USA was $1.9 trillion or $6,280 per person.

The Risk of Obesity

Among obese individuals, triglyceride levels are unusually high, while HDL levels tend to be low; both of these situations are risk factors for heart disease. A recent study involving tissues collected from autopsies of 3000 men (15–34 years old) who had died of external causes (not heart related) identified an association between obesity and coronary atherosclerosis.

Abdominal fat which characterizes obese individuals is also an area of concern. A study of 1300 Finnish men (42–60 years old) suggests that abdominal fat is an independent and major risk factor for coronary events. Several reasons have been suggested for this: a) stomach fat is continually released into the bloodstream in the form of artery-clogging fatty acids; b) abdominal fat also releases compounds that facilitate risk factors such as atherosclerosis, metabolic syndrome and

> **FAST FACT**
>
> A medical study conducted in Finland shows that for every kilogram (2.2 pounds) of increase in body weight, the risk of death from coronary artery disease increases by 1 percent.

Sample Height-Weight Ratios

Body-Mass Index (BMI) relates height to weight in a single number.

Height	Weight Range	BMI	Considered
5'9"	124 or less	Below 18.5	Underweight
	125 to 168	18.5 to 24.9	Healthy weight
	169 to 202	25.0 to 29.9	Overweight
	203 or more	30 or higher	Obese
	Pounds		

Taken from: Centers for Disease Control and Prevention, "Defining Overweight and Obesity," May 22, 2007.

inflammation; c) abdominal fat initiates biochemical events that lead to insulin resistance, a precursor of Type 2 diabetes and heart disease.

Obesity is often a precursor to metabolic syndrome, a dangerous health situation that is manifested through a cluster of symptoms—excess body fat, insulin resistance, low HDL cholesterol, high triglyceride levels and high blood pressure—all risk factors for coronary events. People with metabolic syndrome release immune system messengers called cytokines into their bloodstream. Cytokines lead to a communication breakdown between body cells and insulin which leads to excessive insulin production by the pancreas, creating a situation that is a literal time bomb for heart disease. In addition, this excessive insulin production can raise fibrinogen concentrations in the bloodstream, thus allowing blood to clot more easily, a situation that is a direct risk factor for heart attacks and strokes.

Lack of Activity

Because of their size, obese individuals are more often than not sedentary in lifestyle. Inactivity in and of itself is also a coronary risk factor. Data from more than 88,000 women in the Nurses Health Study shows that a lean sedentary woman had 1.48 greater risks for coronary heart disease than a slightly heavier but physically active woman.

However, the same study also showed that obesity alone is a risk factor, in fact, an even greater risk factor

Many doctors believe that obesity leads to an increased risk of heart disease. (**AP Images.**)

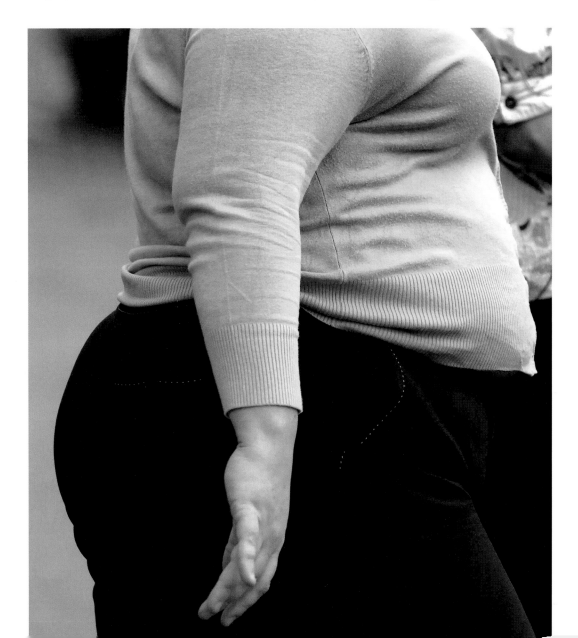

than inactivity because coronary disease risk was highest for women who exercised the least and had the greatest waist-to-hip ratio. The conclusion that obesity itself is a risk factor is also supported by a study of 5881 overweight and obese individuals which showed that being overweight increased the risk of heart disease by 34%, while being obese increased the risk to 104%.

What can we do to help someone we know who is obese or dangerously overweight? Acknowledgement of the problem is the first step. Very often, individuals are in a state of denial about the seriousness of their weight situation. A visit to the doctor or a healthcare professional who deals with the morbidly obese is essential. So are visits to a nutritionist, fitness consultant and body work therapist. Only then can the individual be presented with options viable and necessary for his or her situation.

In severe cases of obesity, surgery would be part of the solution. Lifestyle changes that include exercise and healthy eating are more than essential. Just as critical are bodywork therapies that can uncover some of the real issues behind addictive eating. Learning to read body cues of hunger, depression, stress is equally important for remapping a new life and a whole new cartography of food and consciousness, body and mind.

In Titian's day, the corpulent body was an idealized figure on canvas, essentially exiled to the realm of the fantastic or the realm of the unjust in a society where hunger was the norm. In our days, the corpulent body has its own tale to tell: a Quasimodo [the title character in Victor Hugo's novel *The Hunchback of Notre Dame*] that is both the scourge and product of a culture addicted to perfection.

Body Fat Is Not a Threat to the Heart

Natalie Angier

Fat has gotten a bad rap. That is the unconventional position staked out in the following selection by Pulitzer Prize–winning science writer Natalie Angier. In reality, she says, fat has our best interests at heart. More than just an energy storage medium, it plays a sophisticated role in our bodies, Angier writes. At the onset of obesity, fat cells actually try to resist further weight gain. They do this by releasing inflammatory hormones. If the individual does not get the message, so much the worse for him. In other words, according to Angier, it is overeating and underexercising that threaten heart health, not the fat that results from this imbalance. Angier is a science columnist for the *New York Times*.

In this country, the most popular cosmetic surgery procedure is liposuction: doctors vacuum out something like two million pounds of fat from the thighs, bellies, buttocks, jowls and man-breasts of 325,000 people a year. What happens to all that extracted adipose tissue? It's bagged and disposed of as medical waste; or maybe, given the recent news about socially contagious fat, it's sent by FedEx to the patients' old college chums. But one thing the fat surely is not, and that is given due thanks for serving as scapegoat, and for a job well done.

We are now [2007] in what feels like the 347th year of the fastidiously vilified "obesity epidemic." Health officials repeatedly warn that everywhere in the world people are gaining too much weight and putting themselves at risk of diabetes, high blood pressure, heart disease and other obesity-linked illnesses, not to mention taking up more than their fair share of molded plastic subway seat.

It's easy to fear and despise our body fat and to see it as an unnatural, inert, pointless counterpoint to all things phat and fabulous. Yet fat tissue is not the problem here, and to castigate fat for getting too big and to blame it for high blood pressure or a wheezing heart is like a heavy drinker blaming the liver for turning cirrhotic. Just as the lush's liver was merely doing its hepatic best to detoxify the large quantities of liquor in which it was doused, and just as the alcoholic would have been far worse off had the liver not been playing Hepa-filter in the first place, so our fat tissue, by efficiently absorbing the excess packets of energy we put in our mouths, has our best interests at heart.

"Obesity is not due to any defect in adipose tissue per se; it's an issue of energy balance," said Bruce M. Spiegelman of the Dana-Farber Cancer Institute in Boston. If you are consuming too many calories relative to what you burn off, the body must cope with that energy surplus, he said, "and adipose tissue is the proper place for it."

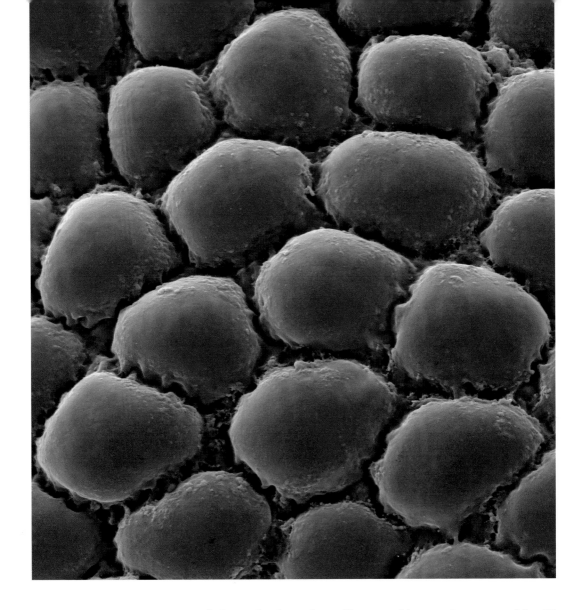

Adipose (fat) cells. (© Dr. Dennis Kunkel/ Visuals Unlimited/Getty Images.)

"If you had no fat cells, no adipose tissue, you'd still be out of energy balance, and you'd put the excess energy somewhere else," he said, at which point really bad things can happen. Consider the lipodystrophy diseases, rare metabolic disorders in which the body lacks fat tissue and instead dumps its energy overruns in that jack-of-all-organs, the liver, causing extreme liver swelling, liver failure and sometimes liver-bearer death.

"Some adipose tissue is a good thing," said Barbara Kahn, chief of the endocrinology, diabetes and metabolism division at Beth Israel Deaconess Medical Center, at Harvard.

Fat Powers the Brain

Indeed, evolutionary biologists have proposed that our relative plumpness compared with our closest nonhuman kin, the chimpanzee, may help explain our relative braininess. Even a lean male athlete with a body fat content of 8 percent to 10 percent of total body mass (half the fat found on the average nonobese, non-Olympic American man) is still a few percentage points more marbled than a wild male chimpanzee, and scientists have suggested that our distinctive adipose stores help ensure that our big brains will be fed even when our cupboards go bare.

Scientists who study fat emphasize that its bland and amorphous appearance notwithstanding, our adipose depots represent highly specialized organs, as finely honed

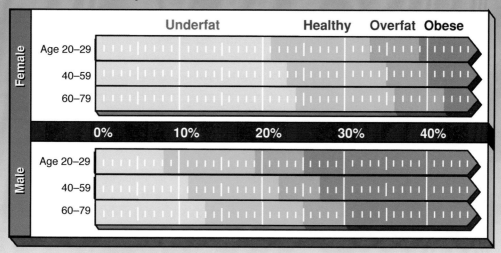

Healthy Body Fat Percentages

The range of body fat percentages considered healthy differs in men and women.

Taken from: QuickMedical, "Body Fat Measurement and Monitoring," Quickmedical.com, 2007.

to the task of energy storage as muscle is built for flexing. Our body fat is made of some 40 billion fat cells, or adipocytes, and their supportive matrix, with most of the bulk stashed under the skin but also threaded viscerally, around and between other organs. Each fat cell is essentially a bouncing balloon filled with those greasy lipids we call triglycerides, three fatty acid chains of mostly carbons and hydrogens arrayed in high-energy configurations that explain why, gram for gram, dietary fat has more than twice the calories of meat or starch; and every fatty acid trio is tacked to a sugar-sweet glycerol frame.

In most body cells, the watery cytoplasm where the labor of proteins takes place accounts for maybe 70 percent of the cell's volume, with another 10 percent given over to the nucleus, seat of the cell's DNA. In a fat cell, by contrast, lipids are king, queen and bishop, and the checkerboard, too. They fill more than 95 percent of the adipocyte volume, crowding the cytoplasm with its proteins and the nucleus with its genes up against the cell wall in what Dr. Kahn calls "a crescent moon space."

Yet for all its lipid density, the average fat cell is ever primed to hoard more, to take in more fatty acids and sugars from the blood and stitch them into triglyceride stores, and to swell to several times its cellular waistline of yore. Most weight that we gain and lose in life is the result of our existing fat cells growing and shrinking, absorbing and releasing energy-rich lipids as needed, depending on our diet and exercise regimens of the moment. But when exposed to chronic caloric overload, fat cells will initiate cell division to augment the supply; and because fat cells, like muscle cells, rarely turn over and die, those new lipidinous recruits will be your helpmeets for life.

Fat Cells Are Active

Fat is no rutabaga. It is dynamic and mercantile, exchanging chemical signals with the brain, bones, gonads [reproductive organs] and immune system, and with every energy manager on the body's long alimentary train.

"We used to think of an adipose cell as an inert storage depot," Dr. Kahn said. "Now we appreciate that it is an endocrine organ," in other words, an organ that like the thyroid or pancreas, secretes hormones to shape the behavior of other tissues far and wide. Squashed to the side a fat cell's cytoplasm may be, but it nevertheless spins out a steady supply of at least 20 different hormones. Key among them is leptin, an essential player in reproduction. Scientists suspect that a girl enters puberty when her fat stores become sufficiently dense to begin releasing leptin, which signals the brain to set the pulsing axis of gonadal hormones in motion.

> **FAST FACT**
>
> Body fat helps regulate body temperature, cushion and insulate organs, and store energy.

Fat also seems to know when it is getting out of hand, and it may resist new personal growth. Dr. Spiegelman and others have shown that with the onset of obesity—defined as 25 or more pounds above one's ideal weight—the fat tissue starts releasing potent inflammatory hormones. That response is complex and harmful in the long run. But in the short term, said Dr. Spiegelman, "inflammation clearly has an anti-obesity effect, and it may be the body's attempt to restrain further accumulation of adipose tissue." The fat sizes up the risks and benefits, and it takes its fat chance.

Prayer May Help in Healing

Duke Medical Center News

Prayer is a global phenomenon, practiced in every major religion. Can it help to heal the heart? In the following selection findings from a study at the Duke University Medical Center suggest that the answer is yes. This press release details the research of Dr. Mitch Krucoff and nurse practitioner Suzanne Crater, whose findings show the use of prayer or noetic therapy may have positive results for cardiac patients. According to the results of their study, patients undergoing invasive catheter procedures did 50 to 100 percent better during their hospital stay when prayed for by seven different religious sects. Patients who received touch therapy, guided imagery, or stress relaxation did 30 to 50 percent better than patients who did not receive such "noetic" therapies. These results suggest that what high-tech medicine needs to perform at its best may be some old-time religion.

SOURCE: Duke Medical Center News Office, "Use of Prayer or Noetic Therapy May Contribute to Better Outcomes in Cardiac Patients," November 11, 1998. Reproduced by permission.

DALLAS, TX—Combining prayer with traditional treatments may offer the best medicine of all, say researchers who tested the power of spirituality to affect the outcome of heart patients undergoing coronary balloon angioplasty.

In a feasibility study conducted by the Duke University and Durham Veterans Affairs medical centers [VAMC], angioplasty patients with acute coronary syndromes who were simultaneously prayed for by seven different religious sects around the world did 50 percent

A Catholic woman prays during Mass. Some studies indicate that prayer may have health benefits. (**AP Images**.)

to 100 percent better during their hospital stay than patients who were not prayed for by these groups.

Other angioplasty patients who received either touch therapy, stress relaxation or guided imagery showed a 30 percent to 50 percent trend of improved outcomes during hospitalization compared to patients who didn't receive such "noetic" therapies, the researchers found.

Intriguing Findings

Although the feasibility study of 150 patients was too small to offer statistically significant comparisons, the results "are highly intriguing, and not what most traditional physicians would have expected," said Duke cardiologist Dr. Mitch Krucoff, who conducted the study with nurse practitioner Suzanne Crater and 22 volunteers. Krucoff and Crater prepared the findings of the trial, known as MANTRA (Monitor and Actualization of Noetic TRAinings), for presentation at the 71st annual scientific sessions of the American Heart Association (AHA).

"Our data show beneficial trends," Krucoff said in an interview. "Our goal was to conduct as scientifically rigorous and reasonable a trial as has ever been undertaken to look at what else, besides pills and procedures, might help us treat patients."

A larger 1,500-patient trial is expected to start soon at five centers: Duke, the Durham VAMC, Scripps Clinic in San Diego, the Washington Heart Center in Washington and Baptist Medical Center in Oklahoma City

FAST FACT

An Israeli study claims that remote prayer can help patients even after the fact. A group of patients who were subjected to post-treatment prayer had better survival rates than patients who were left out of the prayers.

Trial-Tested Prayer and Noetic Therapies

MANTRA was designed to use objective physiological measurements, such as continuous EEG [electroencephalogram] monitoring, heart rate, blood pressure and clinical outcomes, to characterize the effects of spiritual energy in cardiac patients before, during and after invasive catheter procedures. It tested prayer and noetic therapies—interventions that do not use drugs, devices or surgery—on a group of 150 patients at the Durham VAMC. The procedure, which involves threading a tube into the heart while a patient is awake, is used either to collect images of the heart or to clear clogged arteries. It is a procedure that many patients find stressful and which carries medical risks—a population ripe for a little relaxation or other beneficial therapy, the researchers believe.

In the study, Crater randomized the patients into one of five treatment arms. If they received prayer, she sent electronic mail to such sites as Virtual Jerusalem, so that a prayer could be inserted in that city's Wailing Wall, and to Buddhist monasteries in Nepal and France. She called Carmelite nuns in Baltimore, who offered a prayer during that evening's Vespers, as well as Fundamentalists and Moravians. These groups, plus Baptists and Unitarians, all prayed for the patient by name. The study was "double-blinded," meaning neither the patients nor their staff knew of their treatment assignments.

If the patient received a bedside noetic therapy, Crater paired that person up with one of 22 volunteers who either provided guided imagery, touch therapy or stress relaxation.

Without even knowing the results, Crater said the experience she had in offering patients something to help soothe the nerves of patients about to undergo a catheterization was dramatic enough "to change my practice. It is possible to bring a calming, healing space into a hospital, which can sometimes seem cold and sterile." Of the 170 patients she approached to participate in the trial, only 21 were not interested and only one of them refused to be prayed for by a variety of sects. "Most of them were very accepting of these therapies and I think that paid off in their outcome."

Research Backed by Monitoring System

Krucoff and Crater conducted the research with the support of Marquette Electronics in Milwaukee, which provided a unique physiologic monitoring system. They collected information on how the patients did during their hospitalization, which they presented at the AHA, and they collected data on each patient's blood pressure and heart rate during the procedure and hospitalization, which they are still tabulating. They also looked at what happened during the time the 30 patients in each of the five arms was hospitalized. They looked at whether the patient experienced an adverse "event" defined as a heart

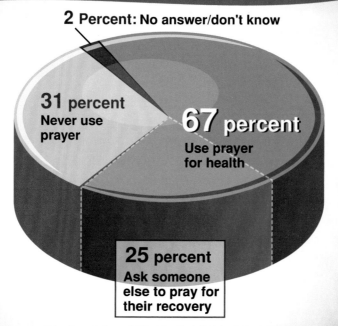

Americans Believe Prayer Helps

A 2001 Gallup poll finds that two-thirds of Americans pray for their health and that a quarter of them ask others to help them get well by praying.

2 Percent: No answer/don't know

31 percent
Never use prayer

67 percent
Use prayer for health

25 percent
Ask someone else to pray for their recovery

Taken from: Gallup poll, "Medicine Finds Religion," March 5, 2002.

attack, death, a second cardiac procedure, pulmonary edema or congestive heart failure.

Findings in the AHA report showed beneficial trends favoring the patients treated with any noetic therapy over standard care. Of the individual noetic therapies, the double-blinded, off-site prayer had the most therapeutic effects, although every noetic therapy had better outcomes than standard care.

"This makes us comfortable that these therapies at least are safe in this patient population, and it suggests that there may be therapeutic benefit, as well," Krucoff said.

Krucoff cautioned that it is important to understand the limitations of any clinical trial design relative to the effect being studied.

Prayer Appears Unhelpful in Healing

William Saletan

Advocates of prayer often claim that studies prove the efficacy of intercessory prayer—that is, prayers made by others for the recovery of a patient. In the following selection William Saletan throws cold water on the idea. Citing what he terms the largest and best study ever of intercessory prayer, Saletan points out that those prayed for not only fared no better than others but actually suffered more complications. He scorns those who attempt to explain away the data. There is a double standard when it comes to the scientific study of religious claims, he argues: If the data agree with belief, they are held as proof; if they contradict belief, they are dismissed. Saletan, with a touch of sarcasm, offers a list of reasons why intercessory prayers might be expected to fail. Saletan is national correspondent for the online magazine *Slate*. The author of *Bearing Right: How Conservatives Won the Abortion War*, he frequently writes on conflicts between medical science and conservative religion.

SOURCE: William Saletan, "The Deity in the Data: What the Latest Prayer Study Tells Us About God," *Slate*, April 6, 2006. Copyright © 2006 Washingtonpost Newsweek Interactive Co, LLC. All rights reserved. Reproduced by permission.

Brother, have you heard the bad news?
It was supposed to be good news, like the kind in the Bible. After three years, $2.4 million, and 1.7 million prayers, the biggest and best study ever was supposed to show that the prayers of faraway strangers help patients recover after heart surgery. But things didn't go as ordained. Patients who knowingly received prayers developed more post-surgery complications than did patients who unknowingly received prayers—and patients who were prayed for did no better than patients who weren't prayed for. In fact, patients who received prayers without their knowledge ended up with more major complications than did patients who received no prayers at all.

Explaining Away the Data

If the data had turned out the other way, clerics would be trumpeting the power of prayer on every street corner. Instead, the study's authors and many media outlets are straining to brush off the results. The study "cannot address a large number of religious questions, such as whether God exists, whether God answers intercessory prayers, or whether prayers from one religious group work in the same way as prayers from other groups," the authors shrug.

Bull. If these findings involved any other kind of therapy, doctors would spin hypotheses about the underlying mechanisms and why the treatment failed or backfired. And that's exactly what theologians and scientists are doing as they try to explain away the data. They're implicitly sketching possibilities as to what sort of God could account for the results. Here's a list.

> **FAST FACT**
>
> In the Study of the Therapeutic Effects of Intercessory Prayer, 59 percent of those who knew that they were prayed for suffered complications, compared with 52 percent of those who were prayed for unknowingly.

1. **God doesn't exist.** This is the simplest explanation, favored by atheists. You pray, but nobody's there, so nothing happens.

2. **God doesn't intervene.** This is the view of self-limiting-deity theorists and of the Committee for the Scientific Investigation of Claims of the Paranormal. God may be there, but He's not doing anything here.

3. **God is highly selective.** The positive effect of prayer on the study's participants "could be smaller than the 10% that our study was powered to detect," the authors suggest. Maybe God heeds prayers, but not enough of them to reach statistical significance.

Prayer Fails to Help

Contrary to his earlier study cited in the previous viewpoint, Mitch Krucoff's more recent study of 748 heart patients, referenced below, found virtually no difference in the number of adverse cardiac events afflicting those who were prayed for versus those who were not.

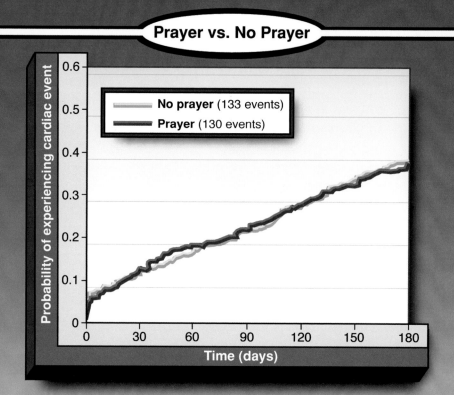

Prayer vs. No Prayer

No prayer (133 events)
Prayer (130 events)

Probability of experiencing cardiac event

Time (days)

Taken from: Mitchell Krucoff et al., "Music, Imagery, Touch, and Prayer as Adjuncts to Interventional Cardiac Care: The Monitoring and Actualization of Noetic Trainings (MANTRA) II Randomized Study," *Lancet*, July 16, 2005.

4. **God ignores form letters.** According to the study's protocol, if you were assigned to pray for patients, the only information you got about them was a daily fax listing their first names and the initials of their surnames. A script told you to pray in each case "for a successful surgery with a quick, healthy recovery and no complications." This cookie-cutter approach may have "impacted the quality of the prayer," according to a scientific editorial that accompanies the study. Form letters don't impress Congress; why should they impress God?

5. **God requires a personal reference.** "Intercessory prayer makes much more sense in community, in family, [where] we're concerned about the well-being of one another," one of the study's authors argued in a teleconference on the findings. A congressman may care whether your lobbyist knows the congressman, but what God cares about is whether your intercessor knows you.

6. **God is unmoved by the size of your lobbying team.** The authors lament contamination from "background prayer" as though it were radiation. Patients "may have been exposed to a large amount of non-study prayer" from friends and family, they warn, possibly swamping "the effects of prayer provided by the intercessors." Evidently, the 1,000 prayers delivered on your behalf by strangers in this study added no discernible effect to the prayers God heard from people who knew you.

7. **God ignores third parties.** Why should God do what a fax from one stranger tells another stranger to ask for on your behalf? The person God's going to listen to is you—and maybe you want relief or salvation more than life. As one author puts it, "What we have in mind for someone else may not be what they have in mind for themselves."

8. **God takes His time.** Maybe the study didn't follow patients long enough, the authors suggest: "The occurrence of any complication within 30 days of surgery may not be appropriate or relevant to the effects of intercessory prayer." When ordering from Heaven, allow at least one month for shipping.

9. **God has a backlog.** Patients' names were faxed to intercessors "starting the night before each patient's scheduled surgery," according to the protocol. Was that too late?

10. **God ignores you if you don't pray hard enough.** "Maybe the people weren't praying very hard," a monsignor tells the *St. Petersburg Times*.

11. **God ignores you if you're wicked.** Responding to the findings, a Baptist pastor cites James 5:16: "The prayer of a righteous man is powerful and effective." No righteousness, no effect.

12. **God helps those who help themselves.** "Many if not most of the wonderful hospitals in this country were built through the intercessory prayers of religious communities of various denominations," a member of the study team observed during the teleconference. "Theirs was the prayer of action instead of word." Deeds, not pleas, save lives.

13. **God does not hear the prayer of a Christian.** The protocol says prayers were delivered by members of a Benedictine monastery, a Carmelite community, and a Protestant prayer ministry. "We were unable to locate other Christian, Jewish, or non-Christian groups that could receive the daily prayer list required for this multiyear study," the authors explain. Oops! Maybe Jerry Falwell had it backward.

14. **God chooses His own outcome measures.** The study measured the effect of prayers on "postoperative complications defined by the Society of Thoracic

A man prays in a hospital chapel. Some studies refute the idea that intercessory prayer can help patients recover. (© Brad Wilson/Photonica/Getty Images.)

Surgeons." But as the accompanying editorial notes, "many prayers for the sick contain the implicit objective of easing the passage of the spirit out of the body, an outcome which, by Society of Thoracic Surgeons definition, would be coded as death." If God doesn't pass your test, maybe you're using the wrong test.

15. **God doesn't participate in studies.** The authors say 1,493 people refused to participate in the study

because they had other priorities or were "not interested in clinical research." Why should God, who has a lot more to do and nothing to learn from a study, react differently? "I don't see him cooperating in a test," opines a Baptist theologian.

16. **God hates being told what to do.** Several clerics argue that the kind of intercessory prayer used in the study is manipulative . . . of divine action and sinfully treats God "as our instrument." The editorial accompanying the study, noting that patients who were prayed for "had worse absolute rates of complications" than those who weren't, asks "whether it was the intercessory prayer per se that may be unsafe." Is the prayer study, like so much in the Bible, a sign of God's wrath? "Researchers must be vigilant in asking the question of whether a well-intentioned, loving, heartfelt healing prayer might inadvertently harm or kill vulnerable patients," the editorial concludes.

17. **God is malevolent.** Patients who received prayers were marginally more likely to develop complications (52.5 to 50.9 percent) and substantially more likely to develop major complications (18.0 to 13.4 percent) than patients who received none. You can't blame the major-complication gap on psychology, since both groups were told that they might or might not be prayed for. In the teleconference, one of the study's authors tried to explain the gap away —"We don't feel confident statistically that that difference is at the level of significance barely that it's actually perhaps real"—whatever that means. But another called it a "possible hotspot," and the editorial warns that in clinical research, "assumptions of Divine benevolence . . . could only be considered scientifically naïve," since "in the history of medicine there has never been a healing remedy that was

actually effective without having potential side effects or toxicities."

Warning: The surgeon general may determine that prayer is hazardous to your health. That's what can happen when faith sets out to prove its power through science.

Driving Cholesterol Ever Lower with Drugs Is Safe

Harvard Men's Health Watch

Most Americans are aware that high cholesterol represents a risk to heart health. In recent decades, a class of drugs called statins has been used to reduce the level of low-density lipoprotein (LDL), the dangerous form of cholesterol, in many patients. In the following selection the *Harvard Men's Health Watch* takes the position that statins demonstrably protect the heart. The publication goes on to argue that the lower the LDLs, the greater the protection. Even in patients who have naturally low levels of LDL, it states, statins produce an extra measure of protection. There seems to be no lower limit on the benefits, and there seem to be no harmful side effects of extremely low cholesterol, it concludes. *Harvard Men's Health Watch* is a monthly publication of the Harvard Medical School, which also publishes the *Harvard Women's Health Watch*.

SOURCE: www.harvardhealthcontent.com, May, 2007. Copyright © 2007, President and Fellows of Harvard College. For more information visit: www.health.harvard.edu/men. Reproduced by permission.

Strict vegetarians don't get any cholesterol in their diets, but they still have plenty of cholesterol in their blood. So does everyone else. In fact, even folks in the burger and fries crowd can trace about two-thirds of their blood cholesterol to their metabolism, not their appetites.

Cholesterol is manufactured in the liver. Diet certainly influences how much your liver produces—when you eat more saturated or trans fat [a highly saturated artificial fat] your liver churns out more cholesterol—but even with a vegetarian diet, regular exercise, and a trim build, the liver produces an irreducible minimum amount of cholesterol. It's a good thing, too, since cholesterol makes vital contributions to health. For one thing, it is a major component of all human cell membranes. For another, it is the building block of steroid hormones, including cortisol, estrogen, and testosterone.

The LDL Risk

Scientists know that cholesterol is essential, but they also know that high levels of LDL ("bad") cholesterol dramatically increase the risk for heart attacks, angina, peripheral artery disease, and stroke. And they have also discovered that reducing LDL cholesterol reduces risk. As studies have accumulated over the past 20 years, the targets for LDL cholesterol levels have steadily declined. For healthy people, an LDL of 160 milligrams per deciliter (mg/dL) was once considered acceptable; now 130 mg/dL is okay, 100 mg/dL, ideal. For people with stable coronary artery disease, diabetes, hypertension, or other major cardiovascular risk factors, the current targets are more stringent still: 100 mg/dL is okay, 70 mg/dL or less, ideal. And for patients with unstable coronary heart disease, it's 70 mg/dL or bust.

Diet, weight control, and exercise are essential for everyone who needs to reduce his cholesterol. But most people need medication to approach an LDL of 100 mg/dL, and virtually everyone needs help to reach 70 or below. Many powerful drugs can provide that help. Most often, doctors turn to a statin drug (see *Harvard Men's Health Watch*, November 2004), but if a statin won't do or if it doesn't do the job by itself, many other drugs are available

Doctors can get your LDL cholesterol way down. But does it really help to get it very low? And is it safe?

Statins Cut Cholesterol

The first statin drug (lovastatin) was licensed for use in the United States in 1987. Five additional members of the group are now available. Although there are some differences among them, they all inhibit the activity of 3-hydroxy-3-methylglutaryl coenzyme A reductase. It's the chief enzyme for cholesterol production; when it's blocked, the liver manufactures less cholesterol and blood cholesterol levels fall. And statins share another important benefit: As cholesterol production falls, the liver takes up more cholesterol from the blood, so levels drop even further.

Having pretty numbers is one thing, preventing disease another. But when the Cholesterol Treatment Trialists' Collaboration performed a meta-analysis of 14 randomized clinical trials of statins, they found impressive benefits. Collectively evaluating more than 90,000 patients for five years or longer, the studies showed that statin therapy reduces the risk of heart attack by 23%, the risk of stroke by 17%, and the overall mortality rate by 12%. Significant benefits were evident by the end of one year, but the gains increased steadily in subsequent years. People who were free of heart disease when they entered the trials enjoyed substantial protection, but people who had already been diagnosed with heart disease by the time they began therapy reaped even greater gains. In addition, the statins were safe, with very low rates of significant liver or muscle damage.

In round numbers, the Cholesterol Treatment Trialists' meta-analysis found that lowering LDL cholesterol by about 2 mg/dL reduces the risk of a major vascular event by about 1%. The greater the reduction, the greater the protection. But the report did not focus on extreme reductions of LDL cholesterol. Fortunately, other studies provide that information.

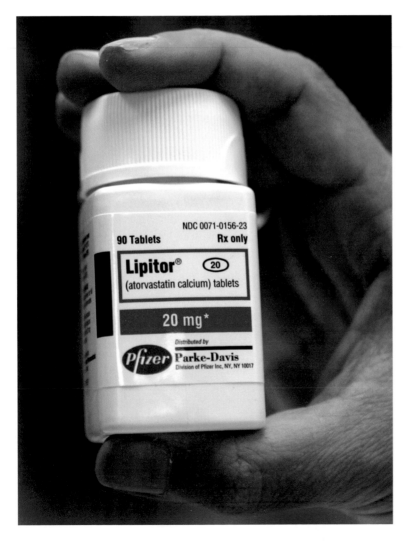

Lipitor is a popular statin prescribed to help reduce cholesterol. (**AP Images.**)

Super-Low Levels

Doctors in Michigan evaluated the benefits of extreme reductions in LDL cholesterol by studying 132 patients with heart disease who had LDL levels of 80 mg/dL, or less before starting statin therapy; their average LDL was just 63 mg/dL. Despite their already low LDL levels, 63 of the patients were started on a statin while the other 69 were not. All the patients had similar risk factors, and they were similar in the extent and severity of their heart disease. Aside from the statins, they also received similar medical therapy. Over six months of observation, how-

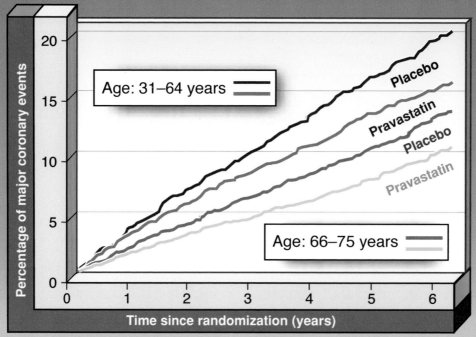

Statins Curb Heart Attacks

This graph from a clinical trial shows that both elderly and middle-aged people who received the statin had significantly fewer heart problems than those who received a placebo.

Taken from: Christopher Raffel and Harvey D. White, "Drug Insight: Statin Use in the Elderly," *Nature Clinical Practice Cardiovascular Medicine*, no. 3, 2006, pp. 318–28.

ever, an important difference emerged: Major vascular events occurred in 29% of the patients who did not get statins but in only 9.5% of the individuals who had extremely aggressive LDL reductions with statins.

Because it involved many more patients and was a randomized clinical trial, a second study is even more convincing. In an earlier report, the Harvard scientists who directed the PROVE-IT trial demonstrated that intensive statin therapy that achieved average LDL levels of 62 mg/dL produced better protection than conventional statin treatment, which lowered the average LDL level to 95 mg/dL. In a new analysis, the researchers divided 1,825 patients into four groups based on their LDL levels four months after an acute coronary event. Ten percent of the patients had LDL levels above 100 mg/dL and 14% had LDLs between 80 and 100 mg/dL, the traditional goal for people with heart disease or major risk factors. But 31% of the group achieved LDLs between 60 and 80 mg/dL, 34% were between 40 and 60 mg/dL and 11% had staggeringly low LDLs of 40 mg/dL or less.

PROVE-IT proved that lower is better, at least for patients being treated for active, acute coronary artery disease. During a follow-up period that averaged two years, 26% of the patients with LDLs between 80 and 100 mg/dL experienced an additional major cardiovascular event such as a heart attack, stroke, hospitalization for unstable angina or an artery-opening procedure, or death. Compared to these patients, those with lower LDLs enjoyed a reduction in major cardiac events.

A Safe Intervention

Even if achieving radically low LDL cholesterol with statin therapy protects the heart, it wouldn't be worthwhile if it damaged other organs. But the PROVE-IT investigators found that extremely low LDL levels were safe, with no additional risk to the liver, muscle, eye, or brain. . . .

The average American man has an LDL of 126 mg/dL Cutting that level in half seems radical indeed, but it may not be. According to a 2004 review in the *Journal of the American College of Cardiology*, our hunter-gatherer ancestors probably had LDLs between 50 and 70 mg/dL—and even today, babies come into the world with LDLs between 30 and 70 mg/dL.

Few American adults can achieve LDLs of 70 mg/dL without medication. It's not a good idea for healthy people who do not have major risk factors to take drugs to achieve very low LDLs, but it's a very important option for people at risk. And if a very low LDL is actually what our human heritage intends, we should all head in that direction by adopting the low-saturated fat, high-fiber, physically active lifestyle that best fits our genetic endowment.

A very low LDL may not be so radical after all.

Driving Cholesterol Ever Lower with Drugs Is Unsafe

Andrew Moore et al.

Cholesterol, especially the low-density lipoprotein (LDL) variety, can be reduced by the use of drugs called statins. This has proven value for those who are at risk of heart disease owing to high levels of "bad" cholesterol in their bodies. Recently, however, various expert panels in the United States and Britain have been calling for an effort to drive cholesterol down to unprecedented levels in the general population by widespread use of statins. While the benefits to taking statins are well documented, risks to health have been reported. Some patients may have pre-existing medical conditions that might cause them to have a greater risk of developing muscle-related problems, including a serious condition called rhabdomyolysis (acute muscle damage). Rare reports of this condition have been connected with the use of these drugs. The researchers at the Pain Research Group at Oxford University, led by Dr. Andrew Moore and Dr. Henry McQuay, found that a small but evident risk of muscle damage is associated with the use of statins.

SOURCE: Andrew Moore, et. al., *Bandolier*, Oxford, UK: Bandolier, 2005. Reproduced by permission.

That muscle problems can occur with statins and other lipid lowering drugs is an accepted problem. While some people seem unable to take statins because of muscle soreness or weakness, the vast majority are unaffected. There is something of a biological progression, from muscle soreness, through more severe muscle problems, to increased levels of creatinine kinase enzymes, to rhabdomyolysis, and even death from rhabdomyolysis (in about 1 in 15 cases).

Most of the spontaneous reports of rhabdomyolysis to the FDA [Food and Drug Administration] were associated with cerivastatin, now withdrawn. The problem with spontaneous reporting is that while it may identify cases, there is always uncertainty about denominators, so rates of adverse events are imprecise. Randomised trials are poor at finding rare but serious adverse events, because the events do not occur in sufficient numbers. Only 12 cases of rhabdomyolysis were reported in 30 RCTs (randomized controlled trials) reviewed.

One way of trying to overcome both these problems is by using large cohort (group of people with common characteristics) studies, where people prescribed a drug, statins in this case, are enrolled in good databases that can identify cases of the adverse events examined. Such a cohort study on statins and rhabdomyolysis is informative.

Study

This was a retrospective cohort study of patients in 11 US health plans providing pharmacy benefits, and with automated claims files covering prescription drugs, outpatient visits, and hospital admissions. Patients with a first prescription of statin or fibrate (another cholesterol lowering drug) were entered, as long as there was no such prescription in the previous six months.

Potential cases of hospital admission for rhabdomyolysis were identified from records of members of the cohort using coded discharge diagnoses. Also used were

claims for measurement of creatinine kinase (an enzyme) within seven days of admission or discharge, or a discharge diagnosis of renal failure plus a creatinine kinase measurement.

Three assessors blind to statin or fibrate exposure status reviewed abstracts of medical records. Rhabdomyolysis was defined as severe muscle injury present at admission, plus a diagnosis of rhabdomyolysis or creatinine kinase more than 10 times the upper limit of normal.

Alice Heckman sorts her medication. She has a history of high cholesterol and heart disease. (**AP Images.**)

Severe rhabdomyolysis was defined as a serum creatinine kinase above 10,000 IU/L or more than 50 times the upper limit of normal.

Results

The cohort included a quarter of a million people with 225,000 person years of monotherapy (treatment with a single drug) for statin or fibrate, and 7,300 years of combined therapy of statin plus fibrate. There was little information for fluvastatin or lovastatin, and these drugs were ignored in favour of the bulk of statin information on atorvastatin, pravastatin, and simvastatin. Fibrate information was much lower than that for statins, and included gemfibrozil and fenofibrate. Within the cohort there were 77,000 person years not exposed to lipid-lowering drugs, during which no cases of rhabdomyolysis were reported.

Thirty-one patients met the inclusion criteria for rhabdomyolysis. Seven of these were excluded because rhabdomyolysis occurred during a period when the prescription records showed that they were not exposed to a lipid-lowering drug. In each case their hospital records showed that they were taking a statin at the time of the event.

Of the 24 events remaining, there were 13 events on statin monotherapy, three on fibrate monotherapy, and eight cases with combined therapy with both statin and a fibrate. Various doses of each statin and each fibrate were being used for monotherapy and combined therapy. Three-quarters of the events were defined as severe rhabdomyolysis. Hospital stay was 1–11 days (average 6). Two patients underwent haemodialysis (procedure to remove waste products from the blood), and one died.

FAST FACT

Some studies show that the risk of heart attack posed by cholesterol goes down as a person ages, raising questions about the appropriateness of widely prescribing statins for the elderly.

Treatment with a Single Drug

There was no difference in rate of hospital admission for rhabdomyolysis between atorvastatin, pravastatin, and simvastatin. The combined event rate was 0.44 per 10,000 person years of exposure, and the one-year number needed to harm (NNH) was 22,700. For cerivastatin, the rate was about 10 times higher, with a NNH of 1,870. For fibrates the NNH was 3,550. Age over 65 years and having diabetes increased the risk of rhabdomyolysis with statin monotherapy, but duration of use made no difference to the event rate.

Combined Therapy

Combined use of statin and fibrate increased the risk of rhabdomyolysis. With atorvastatin or simvastatin plus a fibrate the incidence rate was between 17 and 23 per 10,000 person years, about 40 times higher than with statins alone. The NNH for one year of therapy with atorvastatin, pravastatin, or simvastatin plus a fibrate to produce one case of hospital admission for rhabdomyolysis was 1,670. For a patient aged 65 years or older with diabetes treated with both a statin and a fibrate the NNH was 480.

Combined use of cerivastatin plus gemfibrozil produced a rate of about 1000 per 10,000 person years, with an NNH of about 10.

Conclusion

The problems researchers face over rare but serious adverse events are clear here. Start with a quarter of a million patients and end up with only 24 actual events. Those 24 events include several drugs, at several doses, and given either separately or in combination. And while this is probably the best study of rhabdomyolysis with statins we have, even this has a problem. Seven cases occurred when patients were not on statins according to the prescription analysis, but were on statins according

Statins Can Cause Death

Statins are not without risk. In Canada, every statin on the market is suspected of having caused at least one death.

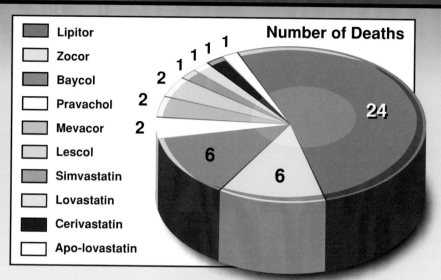

Number of Deaths

Lipitor
Zocor
Baycol
Pravachol
Mevacor
Lescol
Simvastatin
Lovastatin
Cerivastatin
Apo-lovastatin

Taken from: CBC News, "Statins and the Adverse Drug Reaction Database," October 10, 2007. www.cbc.ca/news/background/drugs/statins_adrdatabase.html.

to the hospital records. Fortunately including or excluding the results made no difference.

Despite all these concerns we have some reasonably clear results. Rhabdomyolysis did not occur in the cohort when they were not taking statins or fibrates, as best we can judge. Rhabdomyolysis did occur when they were taking statins or fibrates. We have a reasonable estimate of how frequently the events occurred, both in single and combined use. This allows an estimate of risk of rhabdomyolysis, which is really extremely rare in people taking the most commonly prescribed statins.

With fibrates, or combined therapy, or people more at risk, or with certain combinations (now impossible because one of the drugs has been withdrawn), the risks are higher, or were even common. What we also know is that the risk of dying was even lower. In the 225,000 person years of therapy, even including the withdrawn cerivastatin, only 31 cases occurred, and only 3 of those died. As 10 of the cases were associated with cerivastatin, it would be reasonable to estimate that risk of death with statin, fibrate or combination with drugs commonly prescribed is of the order of 1 per 100,000 per year, and is probably less common than that.

CHAPTER 3

Personal Experiences of Heart Disease

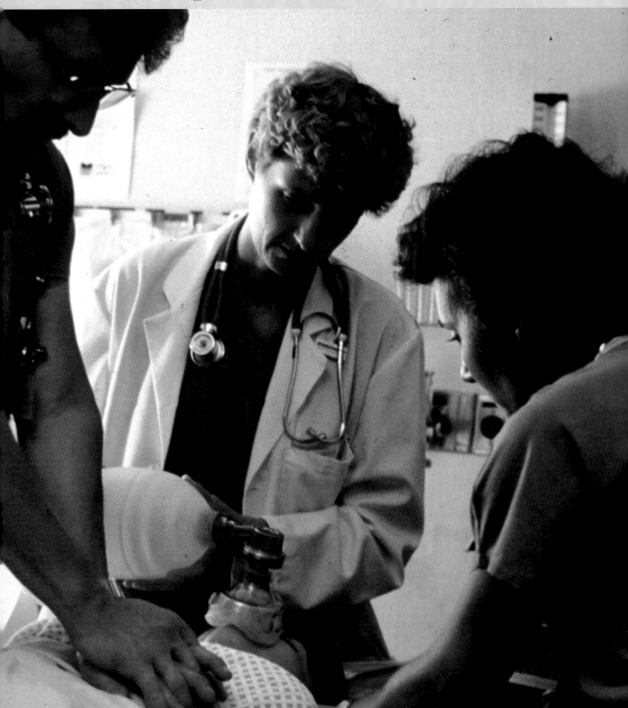

More than You Wanted to Know About My Heart Attack

Helen Smith

Heart disease is commonly thought of as a man's disease, even by doctors. In the following selection Helen Smith tells of a doubly harrowing experience: she suffered a heart attack, but no one believed it. She was treated for everything but what actually afflicted her, and as a result she suffered additional damage to her heart. Smith, an apparently healthy under-forty woman, feels that it was her sex that was the primary factor in her misdiagnosis. Even after the correct diagnosis was eventually made, she continued to suffer symptoms from a malfunctioning heart. She presents her experience as a cautionary tale to others to be aware that heart disease, not breast cancer, is the leading threat to women. Helen Smith is a forensic psychologist who lives in Knoxville, Tennessee.

Photo on facing page. An emergency team treats a heart attack patient. (© 1992 Science Custom Medical Stock Photo. Reproduced by permission.)

A lot of my readers have asked me to tell the full story of my heart attack—so here it is. At the age of 37, I thought I was in great health. I had run regularly from the age of 12, worked as a weight

SOURCE: Helen Smith, "More than You Wanted to Know About My Heart Attack," Dr.Helen.Blogspot.com, October 24, 2005. Reproduced by permission.

trainer at the New York University gym and practiced karate. Although I never thought I was invincible, I had no idea that I would have a heart attack. My family had always had a history of cancer so I figured that if I got sick, this would be my fate (hopefully later on down the line). However, one day I finished working out in the gym and was driving home with my husband when I became short of breath. It was an awful feeling—I felt like I was smothering to death and going to pass out. My husband called 911 and was told to get me to the nearest hospital which he did.

Despite the fact that I was short of breath and shaking like a leaf, the doctor decided I was allergic to something in the gym and gave me a shot of [the allergy medicine] Benadryl. Actually, I later learned that shortness of breath and a sense of impending doom or death were signs (especially in women) of heart problems. I felt ok once I left the hospital and even for a week or two later. I was on vacation in Charleston, South Carolina when I again got short of breath and could not walk. I was so dizzy, scared and light-headed that I spent the day in bed until finally that night, I went to an emergency room. I told the doctors about the allergy reaction that the last emergency room thought I had and they tried some breathing treatments for asthma.

Male Patient Treated Differently

Amazingly, while in the emergency room, a man in his thirties or forties came in with shortness of breath. He was whisked off for heart tests and his wife and two little children were there crying. I felt so sorry for them. Later, I saw a doctor telling his wife that he had stomach problems and his heart was in good condition. If only I could have said the same! The doctors finally did an EKG [electrocardiogram] after I told them that the breathing treatments were not working. The results said that I had a possible MI [myocardial infarction]. A cardiologist came

into the room, looked at the reading and shrugged, stating that many thin women in their 30's who were athletic had a similar reading. I took his word for it and left.

Two doctors and an emergency room visit later, I still had no answer to why I was shaking, short of breath and could barely walk at times from weakness. I thought at times I was having mini strokes. One emergency room doctor refused to look at my abnormal EKG when I came to the hospital; he was too busy dealing with a female coke addict and decided that I was another example of an anxious woman having a panic attack.

A heart defibrillator in O'Hare International Airport. The availability of defibrillators in public places can help save lives. (**AP Images.**)

Tests Reveal Heart Attack

I finally persuaded my regular doctor to quit prescribing me Effexor (an antidepressant) and to look at my heart. He finally sent me for tests. He called back and told me to get to the hospital. My father was with me at the time and took me to the hospital where the orderlies thought he was the one with heart problems and told him to get in the wheelchair. I would have laughed myself silly if I had not been so ill. I had tests, including a heart catheter that helps doctors to see inside the heart. Later, when I was back in my room, the cardiologist came in and told me that I had suffered from a heart attack and also had a ventricular aneurysm (a ballooned out area of the heart) as a result of not resting my heart after the heart attack. I had been told that I had panic disorder so I thought that exercise would be good.

> **FAST FACT**
>
> A Canadian study suggests that heart-attack victims who have high-stress jobs are twice as likely to suffer a second heart attack.

I would like to say that once I got treatment that my problems were over but they had just begun. I was sick with panic attacks for several years. Finally, after more tests in February of 2005, I was told I had ventricular tachycardia [rapid heartbeat] and venticular fibrillation [irregular heartbeat] (which was triggered during testing). A few days later, I received an ICD (implantable cardioverter defibrillator) which is a device that will shock you if you have a serious rhythm problem. I also received the life-saving drug Tikosyn, which is so potent, I had to take it for five days in the hospital to make sure I could tolerate it.

Return of Regularity

For the first time in years, I feel almost normal. I give thanks everyday for the amazing advances in heart research over the past 15 years. I know it sounds cliche, but I feel lucky just to be alive. When other people in their thirties and forties complain about their aches and pains, I just laugh—I feel lucky to get up in the morning without feeling dizzy or nearly fainting.

Women have been led to believe that breast cancer is the number one killer of women. This could not be further from the truth. Almost one half million women die each year from heart disease. Breast cancer kills only 40,000. The sad part is that half of all the women who have a heart attack each year die before they reach the hospital. I believe this is partly because women do not take symptoms of heart attacks seriously—they wait too

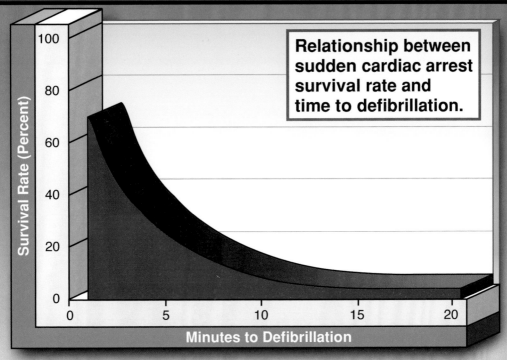

Quick Response Saves Lives

Victims of sudden cardiac arrest are likely to die if they do not receive a reviving shock to the heart within a few minutes.

Relationship between sudden cardiac arrest survival rate and time to defibrillation.

Survival Rate (Percent)

Minutes to Defibrillation

Taken from: MedAlert, "The Med-Alert First Responder Program." www.medalert.com/products.htm.

long before going to the hospital and do not address heart issues with their doctors. Doctors are to blame at times; they buy into the myth that women are more likely to get breast cancer and that heart disease is for men. In order to change this, women must start asking their doctor to discuss heart disease prevention with them from an early age and to demand testing if they have symptoms. Hopefully, awareness of heart disease will infiltrate the public in much the same way breast cancer awareness did—but it will not begin until women decide that red dresses for heart disease are just as important or maybe more so (given the large number of women dying) than pink ribbons are for breast cancer.

An Unforgettable Anniversary

John Kelly

Heart disease is associated with a sedentary lifestyle, typically marked by overeating of fatty foods, smoking, and lack of exercise. In the following selection, however, journalist John Kelly relates his deeply ironic experience: He was felled by a heart attack while in the middle of his regular exercise routine. Kelly had no known risk factors. He was not elderly. He does not smoke. He is not overweight. Nevertheless, while working out on an exercise bike, he began to feel, as he puts it, as if an elephant were perched on his heart. Like many men at the onset of heart attack, he did not immediately seek help (a mistake that often proves fatal, for response time is the single most determinative factor in surviving a heart attack). Instead, Kelly drove himself home. It was his wife who called an ambulance. Once at the hospital, Kelly got the treatment he needed and lived to tell the tale. Kelly is a columnist for the *Washington Post* who focuses on local affairs.

SOURCE: John Kelly, "Survival of the Grateful," *Washington Post*, July 16, 2004, p. C9. Copyright © 2004 The Washington Post. Reprinted with permission.

On March 26, 1658, a surgeon removed a massive kidney stone from the English diarist Samuel Pepys [1633–1703]. The operation involved all sorts of nasty 17th-century medical techniques and by all rights should have killed the patient.

It didn't, and for that Pepys was eternally grateful. He had a special box constructed and kept his stone—the size of a tennis ball—in it. And he resolved to celebrate the operation's anniversary for the rest of his life, which he did, dining with friends every March 26 and toasting his good fortune.

I wish I could be as dramatic as Pepys on the anniversary of the day my life changed —July 17, 2001—but I have no visible souvenir of my heart attack. I just carry a little bottle of nitroglycerin around in my pocket. (Sadly, it's not enough to do any of the fun things one does with nitroglycerin—blow open a safe, knock a hole in a wall.)

Still, whenever the anniversary rolls around, I think back to the summer morning that now neatly divides my life into Before Heart Attack and After Heart Attack.

FAST FACT

Sudden cardiac death during exercise is rare in persons who are apparently healthy. The American Heart Association estimates that, even for heart patients, the incidence of major cardiac events during exercise is no more than one in sixty thousand participant-hours.

Stricken While Exercising

I was at the YMCA, pedaling on an exercise bike, when I found myself bathed in the most disgusting sweat you could ever imagine, like hot, salty motor oil oozing from my pores. My chest hurt and my left arm hurt, as if an invisible elephant was standing on the former and an invisible boa constrictor had wrapped itself around the latter.

I got off the bike, drove myself home and said to my wife, "I think I may be having a heart attack. Ha ha."

She immediately called an ambulance, and I was soon relegated to a supporting role in the drama. On the way to Washington Adventist Hospital, the paramedic said, "Let me get this straight: You thought you were having a heart attack at the Y, and you drove yourself home?"

I grunted in an affirmative sort of way.

"You know," he said, "you really shouldn't do that. We'll pick you up anywhere."

I confess there was a moment when I was being wheeled from the emergency room into the cardiac catheterization lab where I thought This Might Be It. I tried to look on the bright side: I would be able to meet John Lennon and Jesus Christ. I had questions for them both.

But I didn't see a white light, or float above the gurney, or see my entire life flash before my eyes in all its boring detail. I just lay there in a narcotized state while Laurence Kelley, a cardiologist, snaked his way up my offending artery as if he was an explorer piloting a dugout canoe to the headwaters of the Orinoco River [in the

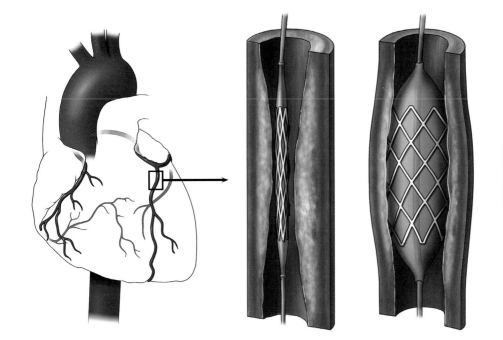

To clear a blockage in an artery a stent may be inserted. First the stent and deflated balloon are inserted into the blocked artery. Then the balloon is inflated and the stent expands. The deflated balloon is then removed, leaving the expanded stent in place.
(© Nucleus Medical Art/Visuals Unlimited/ Getty Images.)

Amazon]. He reamed out the blockage, installed a nifty piece of hardware called a stent and pronounced himself pleased with his work. I then spent four days in intensive care, where I got to have my first sponge bath in approximately 36 years.

No Risk Factors

So, Why me? I didn't have any risk factors, wasn't a "walking heart attack."

Well, why not me? My heart attack taught me that life's not fair. I'd always known this in an abstract sort of way, an ironic oh-I-dropped-my-new-ice-cream-cone on-the-sidewalk-life's-not-fair-wah-wah sort of way. But I didn't know it in a concrete, no-kidding way. I tell ya, one heart attack at age 38 and it tends to drive the message home.

Rather than finding this realization depressing, I decided to find it liberating. If you can die on any day, any day you don't die is cause for celebration.

Which is why tomorrow—barring a too-ironic-for-words death between the time I finish writing this column and the time it runs—I will sleep late, go for a jog, read the paper, putter around the house, hug my kids, kiss my wife, pet my dog (or is it pet my kids, hug my wife, kiss my dog?) and generally take pleasure in the small things that life pretty much gives you free.

At dinner, I will uncork a nice bottle of red wine and toast my good fortune. I think Samuel Pepys would approve.

Leaving the Office

Judi Herring

An old saying has it that an ounce of prevention is worth a pound of cure. In the following selection, physician Judi Herring explains why she left her practice at a university hospital to try to dramatize the need for Americans to take affirmative steps to protect their hearts by preventing obesity. Herring herself literally took steps—embarking on a two-thousand-mile walk with Gary Long, an extremely overweight man who was attempting to get back to health through an extraordinary hike. In August 2006 she left her job and went to Los Angeles to join Long in his walk. Along the way she told him and others about the weight-loss advantages she believes they can derive by eating during a five-hour stretch each day and fasting for the rest. Herring is a urological cancer surgeon. After seeing case after case of obesity-induced medical problems in her clinic patients, she chose to attack the problem at its roots by promoting healthy eating to reverse the obesity epidemic. Herring completed her three-month walk from Los Angeles to Oklahoma City with Gary Long in November 2006.

SOURCE: Judi Herring, "Why I'm Walking," *University of Virginia Magazine*, winter 2006. © Copyright 2007 by the U.Va. Alumni Association. Reproduced by permission.

On Aug. 7, 2006, I left home in Jacksonville, Fla., for a walk. It's September as I write this and I haven't yet returned. My journey is not a personal quest for insight or inspiration, but a public journey intended to bring focus onto a cultural crisis from which many have chosen to look away.

The thermometer in our support car, positioned over the pavement where we're walking, reads 123 degrees. Walking mile after mile across sticky-hot asphalt, I consider that snakes and lizards stay in shade. They can't handle the heat because they can't sweat. My evaporating sweat allows me to remain cool enough to survive in the midst of this sun-fired oven called the Mojave Desert because I am a human with the marvelous ability to adapt to this challenging environment. The combination of the human body and brain has allowed us to survive across the Earth's surface, in the oceans' depths and high into space. The only challenge to which the human body seems unable to successfully adapt is excess fuel consumption: overeating.

Fighting Obesity

This mile I'm walking is one of about 2,000 I will have walked before I return home. I walk with Gary Long, who journals his walk at the Web site www.afatmans journey.com. Aware that complications of his obesity (coronary artery disease, congestive heart failure, diabetes and high blood pressure) were going to kill him, Gary decided to recover his health or die trying. Gary left St. Louis in February 2006 weighing 380 pounds. He walked more than 900 miles and reached New York City in late July. He flew to Los Angeles, where he continues his journey back to St. Louis.

I am not Gary's doctor, nor even his friend. After hearing of his journey from my niece, I called him to explore his agenda. I learned from hours of discussion that we share a common passion: to help solve the obesity epidemic in our country by inspiring and educating one person at a time. On Aug. 18 in Los Angeles, I started walking with Gary as a comrade in arms, a teammate and a supporter. Gary says that his obesity is his problem and he's doing whatever it takes to fix it. I'm saying obesity is every citizen's problem, and we are not doing enough to fix it.

Through millions of acres of scorched wilderness, the strip of asphalt stretches from horizon to horizon, shuttling cars full of people getting their kicks. Yes, it's Route 66. It's hot. I'm sweaty, dirty and walking beside an obese man. We meet countless obese and overweight people, strangers interested in our walk, and we talk with them about our journey and the Fast-5 diet tool (which suggests dieters eat healthily for five hours each day and fast for the remaining 19, thus burning body fat). Many of the strangers' stories are hauntingly consistent as they describe the struggle to combat the impulse to overeat to be demoralizing and defeating. In our casual setting, they openly share stories of the embarrassment of broken chairs and broken beds and the meticulous, time-intensive skin care required to prevent chafing.

> **FAST FACT**
>
> The American Heart Association recommends that adults eat no more than six ounces of meat a day and consume only low-fat dairy products.

A Cultural Malady

Before this walk, I had a comfortable salary as the chief of urology at a university hospital. I traded that for my current salary, which is marked by a single elliptical digit. If this is the future opened to the graduates of [University of Virginia's] School of Medicine, will undergrads still apply?

I hope so, because if we keep trying to attack the problem in the operating rooms and clinics with surgery and drugs instead of taking the battle for health into the trenches where fat happens, our country will continue its self-defeating spiral of overconsumption and snowballing

Steve Vaught, from San Diego, California, stands on a bridge in Little Ferry, New Jersey. He walked across the United States to "lose weight and regain his life." Vaught weighed 410 pounds when he started his journey in April 2005 and had lost more than one hundred pounds by the time he reached New York in May 2006. (AP Images.)

complications. While doctors are busy treating the complications of obesity, more people must fight in the everyday world by educating individuals to make healthy personal choices and to resist reflexively eating food in response to the media blitz that cultivates the impulse to overeat. This cultural barrage sabotages the impulse control required to avoid the consumption of excess food.

Many times in my surgical practice, when I cut into an obese patient's belly with a scalpel, I considered that the real problem in need of a solution was the foot-thick layer of fat I was forcing out of the way to gain access to the surgical goal. My surgical skills would alleviate pain or maintain the patient's life, but would they do anything to address the underlying problem? No. The cure for the illness I fight now is not found in a textbook of medicine or surgery. It's a cultural sickness.

PERSPECTIVES ON DISEASES AND DISORDERS

This 2,000-mile journey is an opportunity to meet many people for whom being overweight and obese are important issues. I learn from them about the challenges they face in their daily efforts to get healthy, and they learn from Gary and from me that there are tools and choices that can help them counterattack the forces that led to their overeating. I left the ranks of traditional medicine and have joined this fight. I walk to educate listeners about diet choices that give power back to people and I encourage them to make life-changing choices.

A Second Attack Changes Everything

Peter Kilfoyle, interviewed by Anushka Asthana

Heart attack survivors usually undergo major changes in lifestyles—but not always. In the following selection, Peter Kilfoyle, member of the British Parliament, explains in an interview how it took a second heart attack to really shake him up. Having realized how lucky he was to survive two potentially fatal episodes, Kilfoyle revolutionized his life. He gave up smoking and heavy drinking and adopted a healthy diet. At the time of his interview, a year later, a thinner and healthier Kilfoyle was embarking on a hike across the Central American country of Nicaragua to dramatize the importance of maintaining heart health. Knowing that hundreds of thousands of his countrymen and women suffer heart attacks every year, Kilfoyle has become a public advocate for prevention through wise lifestyle choices. Kilfoyle has been a Labor Party member of Parliament since 1964, representing a district in Liverpool. Anushka Asthana is a journalist for the British *Guardian* newspaper.

SOURCE: Anushka Asthana, "Interview: 'I Had a Heart Attack. It Saved My Life,'" *The Observer*, September 16, 2007. Reproduced by permission of Guardian News Service, LTD.

If there is one day Peter Kilfoyle will never forget, it is Saturday, 17 June, 2006. It was the day he suffered his second heart attack. He survived.

The sun was beating down on Liverpool and the Labour MP [member of Parliament] wanted to spend the day, a week after his 60th birthday, in his garden mowing the lawn and planting a small tree. Dressed in a scruffy pair of trousers he started to dig, but the ground was so dry and cracked in the heat his metal spade bent in half as he drove it into the soil.

"That was when it started," said Peter last week [September 2007], sitting in his tidy London flat, minutes from [the House of Parliament in] Westminster. "I felt this sensation across my chest and shoulders. I would describe it not as pain but as discomfort. I felt restless."

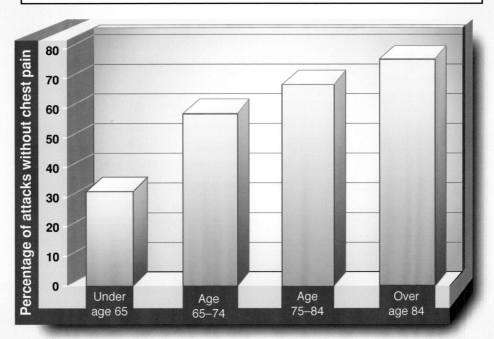

Heart Attacks Can Strike Without Chest Pain

Percentage of attacks without chest pain

| Under age 65 | Age 65–74 | Age 75–84 | Over age 84 |

Taken from: Gail D'Onofrio, "Chest Pain Not Only Signal of a Heart Attack," *HealthLink*, October 22, 2002.

Peter knew he had experienced the same sensation once before, while he was driving along the M40 [highway] heading north from his Westminster office to his constituency in Walton, Liverpool. "I just pulled over and let it pass, then carried on driving," he said, not realising how serious it was.

This time the feeling did not abate. Eventually he decided to drive himself to a local hospital. "I knew something was wrong but I didn't know what," he said. "I thought they might send me away with some paracetamol [pain killer]. My wife wanted to come with me but I said, 'No, you don't want to hang around.' That was how lightly I took it."

It took another 15 minutes to reach the Royal Liverpool University Hospital and when he got there he had to walk up a hill to get to A&E [Accident & Emergency]. All the time the strange sensation that had spread across his upper body continued. It did not take long for a cardiologist to tell him that he had just suffered a heart attack—and that it was not his first. "Just think, you are one of the lucky 50 percent," the doctor told him. "Fifty percent of people who have heart attacks do not make it this far."

A Life-Changing Experience

But Peter has not just survived, he has transformed his life. He Knows, without any doubt, that it was his heavy drinking, smoking and eating that led to the attack and that is why he now walks four miles each day, avoids fattening food, drinks in moderation and never touches a cigarette. He has not weighed himself but his clothes are baggier now and set to become more so this week.

Yesterday [September 15, 2007], little more than a year after he suffered the heart attack, Peter set off from a tranquil Nicaraguan fishing village on a 140-mile trek across the Central American country to raise money for the British Heart Foundation and the Peace and Hope Trust, a local charity. It is a trip he would never have dreamt of before.

Peter knows how lucky he is to have had that second chance. Each year, around 230,000 people in the UK [United Kingdom] suffer a heart attack, one every two minutes, and tens of thousands never make it to hospital. Even he thought twice about going in.

Speaking the day before he flew out to Nicaragua, Peter told how, lying in hospital hours after the heart attack, the only thing that ran through his mind was what had happened to his close friend Mike Carr, who became a Labour MP, then died 57 days later.

"He was an MP for eight weeks and he died of a heart attack after being sent home from hospital," said Peter, taking a deep breath and dropping his head. . . . "I'll never forget that night because they said it was angina and sent him home and then he had another heart attack, which killed him within hours."

Instead, Peter was quickly taken for an angiogram to assess the health of the arteries surrounding his heart. "That was the hardest thing for me personally to face, because I was completely conscious," he said. "They put this tube through an artery right into my body and then released a fluid that enabled them to do a scan on my heart. The results showed that I needed a quadruple bypass urgently." Six weeks later Peter went in for his operation.

Sitting at the dining table in his flat next to a picture of his daughter, Amy, on her wedding day, Peter lifted up his arms to reveal thin red scars running across his skin. He pulled at his shirt and said: "They saw through your breastbone, peel you open and go to work on you, a bit like being a butcher, I suppose." When he first woke up Peter said he was "high" to realise he was still alive and started joking with the medical staff. His surgeon, Aung Oo, later said: "Typical politician—he wouldn't shut up."

Rehabilitation

Peter has nothing but praise for the doctors who helped him through his rehabilitation, but not all get the same

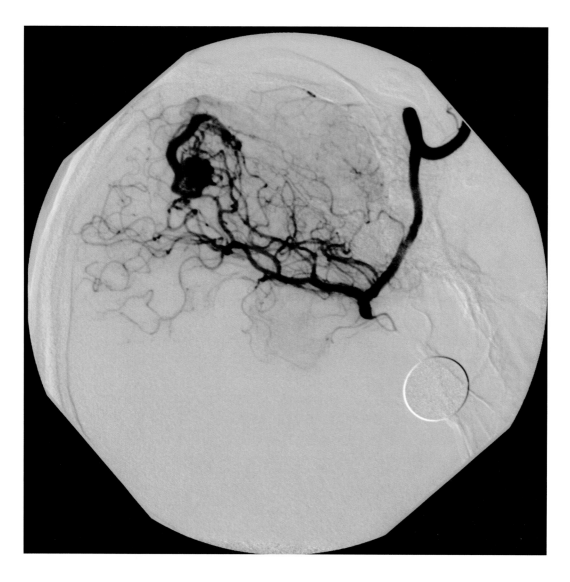

An angiogram showing the blood flow in a coronary artery. (© Adrian Neal/Stone/Getty Images.)

standard of care. A BHF [British Heart Foundation] report this summer [2007] revealed that patients faced a postcode lottery [a method of health care funding in the United Kingdom] after suffering a heart attack, with three out of five failing to gain access to the rehabilitation they needed, such as an exercise programme, advice on lifestyle and counselling. Some were too nervous to get active again and others were dying prematurely, it concluded.

Not so for Peter, who was given the all clear last week for the tough trek he has now started. "I know there are people out there who believe that, once they have a heart problem, they are an invalid for life," he said. "But it just isn't like that with modern surgical and rehabilitation techniques."

During his rehabilitation, Peter and three other men talked to a cardiac nurse about lifestyle. "I got cheesed off with these blokes whingeing [guys complaining] about why this had happened to them," he said. "I told them, I am in here because of one person—me. Nobody asked me to smoke all my life, nobody asked me to drink all my life, nobody asked me to indulge myself with fatty foods."

Peter pointed towards the House of Commons and described his unhealthy lifestyle in what he called the "house of fun". Four days a week he could sit down to a rich lunch and go to two receptions in the evening, all the time smoking up to 40 cigarettes a day.

"I've been in full-time politics now for 20 years and you do spend a disproportionate amount of time sitting around, blowing off about every subject under the sun while stuffing your face with assorted pastries and downing the odd drink or two," said Peter. "You can extrapolate from that into business, into all sorts of professional lifestyles where people sit around, don't get enough exercise and eat and drink the wrong things. I had done no meaningful exercise since I came into full-time politics and I've smoked since I was a kid—40 years."

> **FAST FACT**
>
> A University of Tennessee study shows that walking for exercise regularly for at least nine months helps heart-attack survivors recover both their mental and physical health.

No More Cigarettes

The heart attack forced him to finally give up smoking: "If the choice is between having another heart attack, potentially fatal next time, and having a cigarette you'd have to be a total cretin not to see what the choice is. And even my worst enemies will tell you I am many things, but I am not a total cretin."

He is also eating more healthily, passing on the lunches and receptions in Parliament and drinking in moderation. "We are all allowed one poison and the medicinal value of mother's milk, aka [also known as] Irish whiskey, far outdoes any damage," he jokes. "Seriously, I have spoken to doctors and I am not saying you should drink to excess, but the odd glass of red wine or whiskey does not do any harm."

On his Central American trip, he will cover 10 to 15 miles a day for a fortnight [two weeks]. He will be accompanied by son Patrick, son-in-law Jon Gill, who is a nurse, and fellow MP Greg Pope.

"I am hardly going to indulge in contact sports after my chest has been all stitched up, am I?" Peter said. "But exercise will do you the world of good."

Those who have seen Peter sitting in Westminster bars drinking and smoking may be surprised by the transformation. "Ricky Tomlinson is a friend of mine and he has just been told he has to have the same operation. It is amazing how many people of all age groups are getting this. I don't want to sound like a proselytizer for good health causes, but unfortunately I am because of my own experience."

GLOSSARY

angina pectoris	Pain or discomfort in the chest caused by a reduction in the supply of oxygen to the heart. It is a warning sign of possible impending heart attack.
arteriosclerosis	A thickening and stiffening of the arteries for any reason (often merely the result of aging). Atherosclerosis (see below) is one form of arteriosclerosis.
atherosclerosis	A disease commonly known as hardening of the arteries, caused by cholesterol buildup, which turns into tough plaque on the walls of the arteries.
balloon angioplasty	A surgical procedure for clearing out a blocked artery by inserting and inflating a balloon in the area of the block.
bypass surgery	A procedure to restore blood flow to the heart by grafting a blood vessel taken from another part of the body onto the blocked artery, bypassing the blocked area.
cardiovascular disease	Any disease of the heart or blood-vessel system, such as coronary heart disease, heart attack, high blood pressure, and stroke.
cholesterol	A waxy substance produced by the body and taken in with food that contains meat or dairy products. An excess of low-density lipoprotein cholesterol in the blood leads to atherosclerosis and an increased risk of heart disease.
congestive heart failure	A chronic condition resulting from the inability of the heart to pump enough blood to supply the body's needs. High blood pressure is the leading cause of congestive heart failure.
coronary heart disease	The form of heart disease that results from a narrowing of the coronary arteries that feed the heart, curtailing the supply of oxygen the heart needs.

hypertension	The medical term for high blood pressure, hypertension is a chronic elevation of blood pressure that eventually damages the heart (and other organs), impairing its ability to pump.
lipids	Fatty substances that compose cholesterol. Cholesterol lipids come in two varieties: low density and high density. The low-density lipids (LDLs) cause atherosclerosis, while the high-density lipids (HDLs) tend to counter it.
myocardial infarction	The medical term for a heart attack, characterized by a sudden cut-off of blood to the heart, which deprives it of the oxygen it needs to keep pumping, causing parts of the heart muscle tissue to die.
statin	A class of drugs that lowers cholesterol by reducing its output from the liver and increasing the liver's ability to cleanse cholesterol from the bloodstream.
stent	A surgically implanted ring or tube that serves to prop open a diseased artery so that it can continue to serve the heart.
triglyceride	A form of lipids derived from fat that flows through the bloodstream. In excess, triglycerides may contribute to heart disease.
vascular	Having to do with the body's system of blood vessels.

CHRONOLOGY

B.C.   **Circa 400**   Greek physician Hippocrates identifies obesity as a risk for sudden cardiac arrest.

A.D.   **1538**   Belgian surgeon Andreas Vesalius creates the first accurate drawings of human anatomy.

1616   English physician William Harvey discovers how the heart circulates blood through the body.

1733   English scientist Stephen Hales first measures blood pressure.

1816   French physician René Laennec invents the stethoscope.

1903   Willem Einthoven, a Dutch physiologist, produces the first electrocardiograph, showing the electrical rhythms of the heart.

1912   American physician James B. Herrick first describes atherosclerosis, or heart disease resulting from hardening of the arteries.

1950   Heart disease begins to soar in America as a result of changing diets and lifestyles.

1952   F. John Lewis, an American surgeon, performs first successful open-heart surgery.

1960 Smoking is found to damage the heart.

1967 South African surgeon Christiaan Barnard performs first successful human heart transplant.

1977 A medical team in San Francisco performs the first balloon angioplasty on a coronary artery.

1982 Seattle dentist Barney Clark becomes the first person implanted with an artificial heart intended to last a lifetime. He survives 112 days after the operation.

1987 The effects of high levels of cholesterol in the blood on heart health are confirmed.

2003 A large-scale study shows that heart disease runs in families, indicating that genetic factors are at work.

2007 Specific genetic factors that predispose certain people to heart attacks are identified.

ORGANIZATIONS TO CONTACT

American College of Cardiology (ACC)
9111 Old Georgetown Rd.
Bethesda, MD 20814-1699
(800) 253-4636
www.acc.org

An organization of more than twenty-five thousand cardiovascular scientists and physicians, the ACC fosters professional education, research, and quality standards. It represents its membership in the development of and advocacy for public health policy, especially as it concerns heart disease.

American Heart Association (AHA)
7272 Greenville Ave.
Dallas, TX 75231-4596
(800) 242-8721
www.americanheart.org

The AHA is a private nonprofit organization made up of local chapters around the nation. It works to promote healthier lives free of heart disease and stroke through public education, health promotion, and public policy advocacy.

Centers for Disease Control and Prevention (CDC)
1600 Clifton Rd.
Atlanta, GA 30333
(800) 311-3435
e-mail: cdcinfo@cdc.gov

A unit of the federal Department of Health and Human Services, the CDC carries out research and promotes public understanding of health and quality-of-life issues. Its Division of Heart Disease and Stroke Prevention carries out research and produces publications related to cardiovascular disease.

Framingham Heart Study
73 Mt. Wayne Ave., Suite 2
Framingham, MA 01702-5827
(508) 935-3434
fax: (508) 626-1202
www.framingham heartstudy.org

The Framingham Heart Study is the largest continuous study of a specific population's heart health. Since its inception in 1948 the Framingham Heart Study has produced many major discoveries that have helped scientists understand the development and progression of heart disease and its risk factors. In April 2002 the study enrolled a third generation of participants, the grandchildren of the original cohort from the town of Framingham, Massachusetts.

Larry King Cardiac Foundation
15720 Crabbs Branch Way, Suite D
Rockville, MD 20855
(866) 302-5523
www.lkcf.org

The Larry King Cardiac Foundation was established in 1988 by the famed broadcaster Larry King, who has undergone multiple bypass surgeries to save his heart. The foundation provides funding for lifesaving treatment for individuals who, due to limited means or no insurance, would otherwise be unable to receive the treatment and care they so desperately need.

The Mayo Clinic
200 First St. SW
Rochester, MN 55905
(507) 284-2511
www.mayoclinic.com

The Minnesota-based Mayo Clinic has a reputation for excellence in medicine and for a commitment to health education for patients and the general public. Its Heart Disease Center has a large array of information about cardiovascular illnesses and heart disease.

Minneapolis Heart Institute Foundation (MHIF)
920 E. Twenty-eighth St., Suite 100
Minneapolis, MN 55407
fax: (612) 863-3801
e-mail: info@mhif.org

The Minneapolis Heart Institute's founding physicians recognized that the finest heart care for patients needed to be supported by an enduring commitment to education and research. Together with community leaders, in 1982 they established the MHIF.

National Heart, Lung, and Blood Institute (NHLBI)
PO Box 30105
Bethesda,
MD 20824-0105
(301) 592-8573
fax: (240) 629-3246
www.nhlbi.nih.gov

The NHLBI leads a national program on diseases of the heart, blood vessels, lungs, blood, blood resources, and related concerns. The institute is a component of the federal government's National Institutes of Health.

WomenHeart: The National Coalition for Women with Heart Disease
818 Eighteenth St.
NW, Suite 930
Washington, DC
20006
(202) 728-7199
fax: (202) 728-7238
e-mail: mail@women
heart.org
www.womenheart.org

WomenHeart is a national patient-centered organization that provides support, education, and advocacy for women living with heart disease. It provides referrals to the public, information for public policy leaders and the media, and advocacy on behalf of women's heart health.

FOR FURTHER READING

Books

Albert Howard Carter, *Our Human Hearts: A Medical and Cultural Journey*. Kent, OH: Kent State University Press, 2006.

Mimi Guarneri, *The Heart Speaks: A Cardiologist Reveals the Secret Language of Healing*. New York: Simon & Schuster, 2007.

Kathy Kastan, *From the Heart: A Woman's Guide to Living Well with Heart Disease*. Cambridge, MA: Da Capo Life Long, 2007.

Martin S. Lipsky, *American Medical Association Guide to Preventing and Treating Heart Disease: Essential Information You and Your Family Need to Know About Having a Healthy Heart*. New York: John Wiley & Sons, 2007.

Robert Myers, *Heart Disease: Everything You Need to Know*. Buffalo, NY: Firefly, 2004.

Gerdi Weidner, Maria Kopp, and Margareta Kristenson, *Heart Disease: Environment, Stress, and Gender*. Amsterdam: IOS, 2002.

Julian M. Whitaker, *Reversing Heart Disease: A Vital New Program to Help Prevent, Treat, and Eliminate Cardiac Problems Without Surgery*. New York: Warner, 2002.

Barry L. Zaret, *Heart Care for Life: Developing the Program That Works Best for You*. New Haven, CT: Yale University Press, 2006.

Periodicals

American Academy of Family Physicians, "Anger and Stress Contribute to Coronary Heart Disease," *Science Daily*, October 1, 2007. www.sciencedaily.com. www.cstv.com/sports/m-footbl/stories/082307aci.html.

Associated Press, "Autopsy: USF Football Player Died from Cardiac Disease," August 23, 2007.

Kristen Pixley Denton, "Women Must Take Heart and Take Care of Themselves," *Indianapolis Star*, November 13, 2007. www.indystar.com.

Miranda Hitti, "'Good' Cholesterol Earns Its Name," WebMD, September 26, 2007. www.webmd.com.

John Lauerman, "Antioxidants Don't Cut Heart Disease Rates in High-Risk Women," Bloomberg News, August 13, 2007. www.bloomberg.com.

MedHeadlines, "Fasting May Lower Risk of Heart Disease," November 8, 2007. www.medheadlines.com.

Alan Mozes, "Rheumatoid Arthritis Boosts Heart Disease Threat," HealthDay, November 9, 2007. www.healthday.com.

Nicole Ostrow, "Fasting Once a Month May Benefit the Heart, Researchers Find," Bloomberg News, November 6, 2007. www.bloomberg.com.

Alice Park, "Heart Drugs May Help Lungs Too," *Time*, October 12, 2007. www.time.com.

ScienceDaily, "Life-Threatening Gene Defect Located: Mutation Linked to Thoracic Aortic Disease," November 12, 2007. www.sciencedaily.com.

Todd Starnes, "The Journey Begins: Man Wins Battle Against Heart Disease, Plans to Run Marathon," Fox News, October 23, 2007. www.foxnews.com.

U.S. News & World Report, "Overweight Now a Global Problem," October 22, 2007. http://health.usnews.com.

INDEX